Hapa Girl

Hapa Girl

A MEMOIR

May-lee Chai

TEMPLE UNIVERSITY PRESS
Philadelphia

Temple University Press
Philadelphia PA 19122
www.temple.edu/tempress

Published 2007
Printed in the United States of America

♾ The paper used in this publication meets the requirements of the American National Standard for Information Sciences—Permanence of Paper for Printed Library Materials, ANSI Z39.48-1992

Library of Congress Cataloging-in-Publication Data

Chai, May-lee.
Hapa girl : a memoir / May-lee Chai.
p. cm.
Includes bibliographical references.
ISBN-13: 978-1-59213-615-5 (hardcover : alk. paper)
ISBN-13: 978-1-59213-616-2 (softcover : alk. paper)
1. Chai, May-lee—Childhood and youth. 2. Chai, May-lee—Family. 3. Racially mixed people—South Dakota—Biography. 4. Chinese Americans—South Dakota—Biography. 5. Irish Americans—South Dakota—Biography. 6. Racism—South Dakota—History—20th century. 7. Violence—South Dakota—History—20th century. 8. South Dakota—Race relations—History—20th century. 9. South Dakota—Rural conditions. 10. South Dakota—Biography. I. Title.

F660.A1C38 2007
978.3'004951—dc22 2006032153

110314P

For

Ariel Lien Chai,

Everett Shanwei Chai,

and

Adelaide Ren-Tian Chai

Contents

. . . *hapa* comes from the Hawaiian phrase *hapa haole* (pronounced "hah-puh how-lee") meaning "half-white foreigner." It now describes anyone whose heritage is white plus another racial or ethnic group, but especially Asians and Pacific Islanders. The term is now considered by some to be one of positive self-identification.

—*Asian American Journalists Association Handbook*

Hapa Girl

Prologue

When we first moved to South Dakota, we could stop traffic just by walking down the sidewalk, my mother and father in front, my brother and me trailing behind. Cars and pickups slowed, sometimes in both lanes, and the passengers turned to stare out their windows. Our town was small: just five thousand residents and five thousand students. Apart from the university, there wasn't much to it except tiny family-owned shops, a funeral home, a combination steakhouse–bowling alley, and nine bars.

In the beginning, the stares made my parents laugh. "Now I know what it's like to be famous!" my mother exclaimed, throwing a hand on her hip, another behind her head, starlet-fashion. My brother and I giggled. My father smiled and took her by the arm. He may have nuzzled her neck, he may have kissed her shoulder. "Why shouldn't they stare?" he said. "They think Catherine Deneuve has come to town!"

In those days, when they were still young, my father liked to call my mother by movie star names. Deneuve, Angie Dickinson, Barbara Bain. All the sexy blondes.

At first, I thought people stared because we were from New Jersey. In a town this small, I figured, they must have known we were strangers. I didn't know, at age twelve, that they were staring because they'd never seen a Chinese man with a white woman before, and a blonde woman at that. I didn't know they thought we were brazen, flaunting our family in public. It was 1979, and we imagined that the segregated past was just that, past. Later, it wouldn't seem so funny. The stares made me feel as though I'd forgotten to put my clothes on. I could feel their gaze rub across my skin. After men started driving by our house to shoot, after our dogs were killed, it wasn't funny at all. By then my father had stopped calling my mother by movie star names. And my mother had stopped making jokes.

1 The Wearing of the Green

I'll begin where I'm happiest, or most clueless—either adjective could be equally appropriate. I'm a child, eight, maybe nine, years old, living in the suburbs, part of the megalopolis twenty-five miles outside New York City, where my father is chair of the Asian Studies Department at City College.

It was my parents' wedding anniversary. As this was also St. Patrick's Day, our house was filled with the scent of corned beef and cabbage. And I do mean filled—from top to bottom, every inch of every room permeated. There was no escaping the pungent vapors, not under my bed, or in the closet, or even in the upstairs bathroom with a towel rolled up and stuffed against the bottom of the door. I know because I'd tried them all.

For more ordinary occasions my father might have preferred Chinese food, but on this day only the most Irish of dishes would do. It was a time for celebration. Chinese was for everyday.

My brother and I were eating our TV dinners in the family room, watching sitcoms or reruns of *Star Trek,* while our parents dined together privately in the kitchen. Candles on the table, fresh roses in a vase on the counter. We could hear them laughing together, excluding us. Sharing private thoughts. Secret things. Normally, we might have been jealous. On any other occasion we might have caused a ruckus just to get their attention, but for their anniversary we had to be good. This was the one and only night when they were allowed to be a couple and not just our parents.

Still, it was disturbing to my brother and me that our parents could sound so happy without us. Our egos didn't like the implication at all.

They were going to see a movie after dinner. A revival of *It's a Mad, Mad, Mad, Mad World.* They'd first seen the film on their honeymoon and they remembered it as the funniest film ever made. Back then, in the 1970s, there was no such thing as VCRs, so they hadn't been able to see it for years. Now they were leaving my brother and me behind so they could relive the moment. My brother and I pretended we didn't mind. We didn't want to see that old movie anyway. Who cared if it was the funniest film in the world! There was going to be a Western on TV. What could be better than that? I had my six-shooter ready, my brother his feathered headdress, we were all set to play along with the film. My brother always sided with the Indians in those days. Me, I was gonna be John Wayne.

My mother came in to check on us before the babysitter arrived. She was wearing a clingy red dress and a long string of onyx beads around her neck. Her hair was piled high upon her head, and when she kissed my little brother good-bye, her lipstick left a red halo on his cheek. She smelled like perfume and hair spray, and when she hugged me, I could almost forget the boiled cabbage. Was there ever any scent as glamorous as Chanel No. 5 and Aqua-Net? I wanted to rub my mother all over my arms. I wanted to smell exactly like her. Sophisticated and grown up and happy and in love.

Then my father was standing in the doorway to the family room, pointing at his watch impatiently. He was wearing a good suit, Brooks Brothers, with a green silk handkerchief in his breast pocket and a green stripe in his black silk tie, in honor of my mother and St. Patrick.

"Hurry up, we're going to be late!"

"I'm saying good-bye to the children!"

"Hurry up, hurry up!"

My mother turned toward us, and for a second worry flitted across her face. "Don't let any strangers in. And don't tell anyone your parents are gone if anyone calls on the phone. And don't let the babysitter invite her boyfriend over."

"Hurry, hurry!"

The doorbell rang, the babysitter. My mother kissed us both goodbye again and then she and my father disappeared.

After they were gone, the house no longer seemed full of secrets, just cabbage, and my brother and I gave the babysitter a hard time because we didn't like to be abandoned.

As we squinted at John Wayne fighting his way across the plains, I imagined my parents laughing uproariously at the Funniest Film Ever Made. I could see my father with his head tilted back, tears springing from his narrowed eyes, and my mother holding on to his arm as she gasped for air. I knew how they laughed together when they were happy—and I felt bitter. I convinced the babysitter that our parents didn't mind if we let the dogs into the family room and later I told her, no, my brother and I didn't have to go to bed, we were allowed to stay up as late as we wanted.

"You're gonna get in trouble," my brother mouthed to me. He was a year younger and very obedient in those days.

"It's St. Patrick's Day," I retorted. "It's special."

But when our parents did arrive home, they weren't angry, even though our Siberian Husky had missed the newspaper we'd put on the floor for him. The babysitter had cleaned it up, but she told our parents immediately even though I'd made her promise not to, and my father gave her an extra tip before driving her home. I'd thought my father would be upset, and any other night he would have been, but this night nothing we did could ruin our parents' happy anniversary mood.

"I'm so glad you kids are still up," my mother said. She sat down between us on the family room sofa, slipping her feet from her pumps and propping them upon the coffee table. She wiggled her toes. "I missed you."

"Really?" I forgave her for abandoning us.

When my father returned, he was still hyper, maybe wanting the day to last a little longer. "Let's watch some movies," he said, rubbing his hands together.

"There's nothing on TV," I pointed out, and there wasn't. Only a rerun of *Love, American Style,* which my brother and I hated. "You missed everything."

"No, no, I mean *our* movies," he said.

And so he ran to the basement to set up the movie screen while my mother made my brother and me change into our pajamas. Then the three of us sat in folding chairs on the far side of the ping-pong table, while my father ran the projector and showed us the honeymoon reels of my parents' trip to Niagara Falls.

The Super-8 footage was already worn by this time, and it had caught on fire once, bubbled and split, but my father had spliced it together again so that it only jumped a little. There were my parents dancing together in black and white, my mother in her long, off-the-shoulder, backless evening gown—which I knew was a deep green velvet—my father in a slim black tuxedo. They whirled round and round, faster and faster, as people in the background clapped. And then the camera zoomed in on an elderly Chinese couple seated at a dinner table, my father's parents, my Ye-ye and Nai-nai, and they were clapping most furiously of all. From a corner, my father's middle brother waved. I recognized my uncle immediately, although he was older now and his glasses were different. My father's entire family had accompanied him on this part of the honeymoon, which my grandparents had paid for. They were all so excited to be welcoming a bride into the family.

"Where's Uncle Alvin?" my brother asked.

"He's taking the pictures," my father explained.

There were more shots: shaky images of clouds, then water, as my uncle experimented with some art-house photography. My parents and grandparents standing on the deck of a boat, everyone covered up in raincoats, the giant falls rushing behind them. They smiled and waved, smiled and waved. In the flickering light, the projector humming, my brother curled into a ball and fell asleep, but I watched the screen without blinking. I loved these movies of our family. My parents dancing like giants on the screen, my grandparents beaming, as the camera zoomed closer and closer, until their smiles were literally three feet wide.

When the film ran out with a click, the screen filled with a blank square of white.

"One more time," I insisted.

"It's late. It's time for bed."

"Please!"

"All right. One more time."

My father threaded the film through the reels again, because in truth he was proud of these home movies too, and I sat up straight in my chair, ready for my movie star parents to flood the screen once more.

2 The Sexy Artist Meets the Boy from New York City

One of the rumors floating around town in South Dakota, as people began to speculate about my parents, was that my father was a white slaver. He must have somehow kidnapped my mother and forced her to marry him. Why she didn't just up and leave, since she was equipped with a car, a career, and access to us kids, didn't seem to pose any particular mental obstacles for people inclined to believe this scenario. Another rumor was that my mother, being a good Christian lady, had been hoodwinked into marrying a heathen in a rather naive attempt to save his soul. Other people preferred to ignore my father—and my muscular brother—and claimed that my mother was a saint for having adopted one of those poor Vietnamese boat people, just like the ones they'd seen on the TV news—in other words, me. Perhaps my mother and father had then found each other, as though by accident, like Mr. and Mrs. Brady on *The Brady Bunch*, and somehow we became a family, without any sexual hijinks that would have led them to actually procreating. In our town, it was not uncommon for cousins to marry, generation after generation, so perhaps this asexual television sitcom version of our family made more sense than the unimaginable notion of marrying not only outside one's race but outside one's family circle.

(Family values were indeed abnormally strong in our town, I came to realize as the years passed.)

My parents actually met at an art exhibit in Southern California, where my father fell in love at first sight, bought one of my mother's watercolors, and made his move. Fast.

"I was a New Yorker," my father liked to say as he would recount the story to my brother and me. "I knew how to *operate*."

My mother had been invited to show some of her watercolor paintings at an art exhibit on the grounds of the University of Redlands. She'd been the director of news and publications there for many years and had organized and led the school's study-abroad program to Mexico. She'd painted these watercolors on the last program she'd supervised, in Guadalajara and Mexico City to study art and archaeology. My father, newly arrived from Manhattan to assume his first tenure-track teaching position, was being escorted by the dean around the pretty, quiet campus when they stopped to admire the artwork.

My father liked to tell this part of the story. My mother was dressed in a mauve knit dress, standing barefoot. It had been a long day, her boyfriend of four years was supposed to have come and picked her up by now, but he was late—as usual—so she'd kicked off the pointy-toed heels that were in fashion in those days and let her toes wiggle freely in the lush green lawn. It was early October and the afternoons were still warm in Redlands.

A sexy artist! my father thought, eyeing those bare toes.

The dean introduced them. The new political science professor from New York City, Winberg Chai. The artist, Carolyn Everett.

In those days, my father wasn't yet seen as the Chinaman, nor my mother as the White Woman, the Blonde. In fact, she wasn't blonde yet. She'd recently dyed her hair a cherry-mahogany color that caught the slanting rays of the sun and seemed to glow and pulse with red light.

My father bought one of her paintings immediately. A watercolor in heart-stopping reds, vermilion tile roofs and vibrant gardenias, azalea blooms and blazing sunlight, all from a village my mother had visited outside Oaxaca.

"Have you been to Mexico?" my mother asked.

My father shook his head. He liked all the reds in the painting, he explained. A good luck painting. A my-heart-is-beating-just-for-you painting, he thought but did not say.

My mother smiled. "For you," she said, "half-price."

How could she have known that nothing was so dear to my father as a bargain? He was smitten. There was no turning back now.

"I would like to invite you to a tea I am holding," he said formally. "For the foreign students. Please put your name and phone number on the back." He gestured to the painting my mother was wrapping in newsprint for him.

The dean was surprised by my father's boldness. My mother, too, but she complied, which surprised her even more when she thought about it later. In fact, even my father was surprised by his boldness. But he knew. He had found the one woman for him. He was in love.

He'd waited thirty-four years to find a bride. In New York, it had been impossible. First, because of his career. How could he support a wife and family of his own while a student, especially when he donated part of his salary every month to his parents, for their use and for the stipends they sent back, hidden in the pages of magazines, sewn in the hems of garments, rolled into balled socks, to my grandmother's family left behind in China? My grandmother's family had been doctors who hadn't cared about politics, who didn't care if the government was run by the Nationalists or the Communists. They figured China would always need doctors. So they hadn't fled to Taiwan before 1949 as my grandmother had advised. They'd been wrong, of course. They hadn't realized the Communists would decide China didn't need doctors, especially Western-educated ones, and now they lived off the secret dollars my grandmother smuggled to them, which they traded on the black market that everyone pretended did not exist.

Second, it had been impossible to find a bride because my grandmother had decided to spend her days in exile in New York as a matchmaker. Using my father as bait, she'd lure the best families in Taiwan—generals and politicians, professors and college presidents—into sending their daughters to visit her in Manhattan and meet her eligible first-born son, the Ph.D., the tall one, all of five foot eight, which after the deprivations of the war years was tall indeed. But then my grandmother would send my father away and introduce these charming young women in their shiny new *qipaos*, in their expensively coiffed hairdos, their perfectly made-up faces, to other eligible young men who were studying in the States and who, of course, were also from other very good families from Taiwan. My grandfather, Ye-ye, would cook all afternoon in the kitchen, providing the dim sum, the stir fry, the snacks and seeds, the buns and noodles, while my grandmother, Nai-nai, laid out American board games—Twister and Parcheesi, cards and checkers—to break the ice, while all these young people paired up and flirted.

This way, all these good families would be indebted to my grandmother. She presided at the weddings, the guest of honor. Sometimes my grandfather even walked the brides down the aisle if their fathers were unable to obtain visas to come to America. My grandmother was toasted by both bride and groom at every wedding banquet. Their parents sent her gifts, scroll paintings and bolts of silk cloth, but mostly she collected their gratitude, the promise of debts she could call in if necessary. My grandmother understood how the world worked.

Unfortunately, her activities meant that my father had to remain unmarried. What good was the bait if he was already hooked? And a first-born son with an American Ph.D. and a green card from a good family—and let's be honest, my grandmother knew just what a good family she had—was the very best bait of all.

But now my father was three thousand miles away. He was on his own. And he'd fallen in love with my mother at first sight. He found out everything he could about her from the dean—in addition to being an artist, she'd been a broadcast journalist, had her own interview show with the local NBC affiliate. She'd worked around the clock as the news bureau chief for the university before deciding just that year to leave the rat race and teach, becoming the head of the art department of a local junior high school.

That very evening my father called my grandfather in New York, even though it was midweek and he usually saved expensive long-distance calls for the weekend when it was less painful for his teacher's paycheck.

Naturally, my grandfather was surprised to hear my father's voice. "Winberg, is everything all right?" Ye-ye shouted into the receiver.

"Sssh," my father whispered into the phone.

"What is it?" Ye-ye answered in a hushed voice. My grandfather was losing his hearing, and my father hadn't wanted him to shout his news across the apartment, where his mother and quite possibly his younger brother were seated on the couch before the television. He knew his family's habits.

"Ba, I've met someone."

Ye-ye was delighted and immediately called out, "Don't worry about the tenure committee just yet! You've got plenty of time!" just to throw Nai-nai off the trail. Ye-ye understood my father's dilemma quite well. Then he whispered, "Who is she?"

My father told Ye-ye everything he'd learned, that this woman was an artist, a writer, a teacher, someone who'd hosted her own television interview show. She was beautiful. And she was kind. He explained how she had given him a discount on the painting. He could hear his father sigh at the other end of the line.

"Perfect," Ye-ye said. "I will send you some gifts for her immediately."

And my father knew then that his father was on his side.

The only problem remaining, besides Nai-nai, would be to convince this woman, Carolyn Everett, that she wanted to marry him.

It took my father five months, the longest five months of his life, he later claimed, but after taking her to the Los Angeles opera, to the symphony, to movies, after endless bouquets sent to her school, outings to the beach and to a wooded mountain park nearby known as Oak Glen—trips always chaperoned by one of her many younger sisters—she agreed to consider my father's proposal.

My father began to sweat heavily and had to take three or four showers a day. He lost his appetite and started losing weight. He became so thin, in fact, that Carolyn grew worried and began cooking meals for him, but the intimacy of a home-cooked meal after months of La Choy only made him more anxious. What if she refused him?

Carolyn was quite choosy, my father discovered. He learned from her little sisters that many, many men before him had proposed to her and she had turned them all down. One man, a former football star, had been deemed too athletic.

"I hate sports," my father pointed out quickly.

Another man was a Methodist and had insisted she convert. Carolyn, a staunch Catholic, had refused and broken up with him.

"I can become a Catholic, no problem," my father told her.

Yet another suitor, a wealthy man, a fellow artist, had begged her to marry him for years, but he didn't want to have any children.

"We'll have beautiful children," my father promised. And then, improvising, he cried out, "And we'll go have ice cream on Sundays!" (Although my father did not actually eat ice cream, he thought this seemed like a homey, American thing to do.)

Finally, after five months of my father's constant attentions, my mother agreed to marry him.

My father used to laugh at his own audacity when I was a small child. He insisted that my mother had married him because of his charm. "I was really slick back then," he'd say and laugh some more.

My mother did not disagree about my father's charm, but she remembered things a little differently. She had been annoyed that afternoon of the art show as she waited for her boyfriend of four years, a fiancé of sorts, really, because everyone expected them to marry and he'd proposed many times, although they'd never set a date. It was getting late and she'd been standing all day, chatting with students, with her former colleagues at the university, with the other artists. By late afternoon her feet were aching, everyone else was leaving, and there she was stranded without her car when the dean came by, smiling and waving with this new professor from New York City.

The first thing my mother noticed about my father was that he was skinny. The second thing was that he looked too young for her. Later, it startled her that she had thought of such a thing, had appraised him that way. After all, she was mostly taken. She wasn't in the market for a man. But her boyfriend was late again, and she was angry, and maybe that was affecting her judgment.

Then, when this young man wanted to buy her painting, why had she spontaneously offered to cut its price in half? What had she been thinking? She didn't have much money to spare, in fact. She was the oldest of eight children, her father and mother were still struggling financially as her father had fallen off the wagon recently, as people said in those days, and so it was she who paid for her six younger sisters when they needed little things that my grandmother couldn't see the point of, things like guitar lessons and dance classes, voice and art classes. On weekends she took the youngest girls, still in their early teens, to the beach and cooked a special kind of chili she had invented just for them on a hibachi half buried in the sand. She shouldn't be turning away money. But my mother had a kind heart, and there was something about this young man that made her want to give him the painting.

Her boyfriend, in fact, was a millionaire. But my mother was used to dating wealthy men—artists and musicians, mostly. She seemed to attract them effortlessly and they fell in love with her, too, and begged for her hand in marriage. But, for many reasons, she hadn't married any of them. One liked ball games and skiing; she did not. Another had a male roommate who seemed just a little too jealous whenever my mother and her pianist boyfriend went on a date. A third was melancholy and cowed by his Mafia don father. A fourth had refused to convert to Catholicism. The others were lost to memory by the time I was born, so I cannot say exactly what went wrong, although I do remember my mother mentioning one man whom she had liked just fine until they went to the beach together and she observed for the first time the way the sunlight glinted off the thick, furry blond hairs that covered every inch of his body. That man, she'd said, was nice enough but utterly repellant sexually.

That evening, after my mother's boyfriend finally arrived and helped her take down her easels and pack everything into the trunk of the car, she made him supper as usual and he talked about himself as usual and my mother could not get the image of my thin father out of her mind. And then, as she washed the dishes, her boyfriend, with a familiarity that made her blood boil, opened up her refrigerator and drank the entire carton of orange juice that she had just purchased for the week. He opened it, tilted back his head, drank straight from the carton, threw it away, and burped.

My mother turned from the sink, her fists on her hips. "That was my orange juice."

Her boyfriend stared as though she were speaking a foreign language.

"You drank my orange juice. That was supposed to last me all week."

He laughed then. "You can always get more orange juice."

Furious, my mother turned her back to him and faced the sudsy dishes. She couldn't actually buy more orange juice. Not until she got paid at the end of the month. She'd already paid for her sisters' music lessons, her rent, her groceries, and her art supplies; there was nothing left over. She wanted to cry and she wanted to break something at the same time. That was the problem with millionaires, she realized. They were selfish, and they didn't know the value of money.

When she felt calmer, she turned back to her boyfriend. "I've been thinking. We should start seeing other people. You should start dating other women."

"I don't want to date another woman," her boyfriend protested. "Don't be crazy. I love you."

"Well, you should think about it. Because I'm going to start dating other men." Then my mother escorted him to the door.

But my mother was not sure at first about dating my father. And certainly even less sure about marrying him, although he proposed after their very first date, which she found both disconcerting and presumptuous.

Even after months of my father's best efforts, she was still unconvinced. Sure, my father was generous, they shared the same interests, he didn't mind when she brought her little sisters along on their dates, he wanted children himself—whereas the millionaire had been stingy, stodgy (she could see that now), and every time she mentioned children he would argue that it was cruel to bring another life into this uncertain world. But marriage? What did a few months mean when contemplating spending the rest of her life with this man?

My maternal grandmother tried her best to persuade my mother to marry my father. What difference did it make that he was skinny or young-looking or from that faraway city in New York? He was in love. Love shouldn't be discounted, Grandma insisted. It had gotten her through all the rough years, all the drinking years, all those long sleepless nights filled with shouting and broken glass and crying children. Love had sustained her despite everything.

In fact, my grandmother had been worried for years that her eldest daughter—already thirty-two and unmarried—was going to join a convent again (my mother had entered a nunnery at age seventeen, decided she disliked the silence there, and left the same day) or, worse yet in my grandmother's eyes, remain a spinster. In 1965, my grandmother could think of no worse fate for a woman.

Finally, in December, my mother told my father that she would give him her decision soon. It had been cruel of her to string him along, she said. He'd been spending so much of his (meager) salary on tickets to the Los Angeles Symphony, the opera, dinners out, the constant stream of bouquets. She would give him her answer that very week, but first she would have to pray about it.

"Sure, sure," my father agreed. "We'll both pray."

After that, my father said he'd never prayed so hard in his life, not even during his childhood in China when his family had hidden in caves while the Japanese bombed their city.

As my father drove my mother to Mass that Sunday, he had never been more nervous. They arrived at Sacred Heart Church a little late. My father couldn't concentrate and made a wrong turn and then another. He could navigate around Manhattan with no problem, but he'd never been able to find his way in a small town. It didn't help that he was sweating so profusely his hands had slid from the steering wheel.

There was no more time to talk as they headed up the steps of the church, my mother adjusting her black lace veil carefully, my father desperately wiping his sweating palms on his pants one more time.

Had any Mass ever lasted so long as this one? It seemed as though every rite was performed twice, the monsignor's homily could have filled a book, an endless procession of people went up to receive Communion—the line snaked up the center aisle, pooled in the back of the church, and continued up the stairs to the choir balcony. Being a recent convert to Catholicism, my father hadn't realized how seriously the Catholics took Advent.

After Mass, my mother continued to kneel, her hands pressed together in prayer. My father knelt beside her now. This might be the last time he would ever be so close to the woman he was convinced was his soul mate, and he felt quite sad. But he also resigned himself to his fate. He had used every trick he possessed to try to persuade this woman to marry him, and if he had failed, there was really nothing more he could do. He grew calmer, almost Zen-like in the acceptance of his fate. He closed his eyes and tried to live in the moment, memorize every second so that he would be able to recall it later when he was old and alone and unhappy: the smell of my mother's perfume—a delicate scent of lilacs and lily of the valley—the rustle of her skirt, the faint hush-hush of her breath, when suddenly he heard her gasp.

My father opened his eyes.

My mother was staring at something in her palm. "Look, Winberg!" She held up a tender red rose petal for him to see.

They both peered into her hand carefully. It was indeed a rose petal. There were no roses in the church. Poinsettias, yes—white and red, in green foil-covered pots—but no roses. It was December, no roses were blooming outdoors. My father had just cleaned his car, knowing he would be taking my mother to church, so it seemed unlikely the petal had been picked up from the seats. Besides, it was fresh and moist, not dried and crumbling, not something left over from last week's bouquet.

"It's a miracle," my father suggested, hopefully. "It's a sign."

My mother nodded.

And that week they made it official, announcing to my grandparents on both sides, and to the entire town, that they were getting married.

The only hint of trouble came when the president of the university called my father into his office. My father was prepared for more congratulations, but the president was frowning and tapping his dry fingers in an odd way atop his desk blotter, as though trying to kill invisible ants swarming his desk.

"About your engagement, Win," he said with forced jocularity.

"Thank you," my father said, misinterpreting him entirely.

The president cleared his throat nervously. "It's just . . . wouldn't you be happier with a Chinese girl?"

"Oh, but Mr. President," my father said, for he was very polite when he was a young man, especially before he had tenure, "you told me when I came here that I couldn't date the students, and the only Chinese girls here are my students!"

"Why, yes," the president said, and suddenly his whole tone changed. He spoke briskly now, sensing the even deeper trouble he could have gotten the university into. "Carolyn is a fine girl. A wonderful person. Just beautiful. I'm sure you'll both be very happy."

"Thank you, Mr. President," my father said, and the president never brought up his concerns again. In fact, after my parents' engagement announcement appeared in the *New York Times,* the president and his wife gave my parents a very nice wedding present, my father said. Something silver and expensive. Engraved. Something that said, "Let's just forget about our little conversation, shall we?"

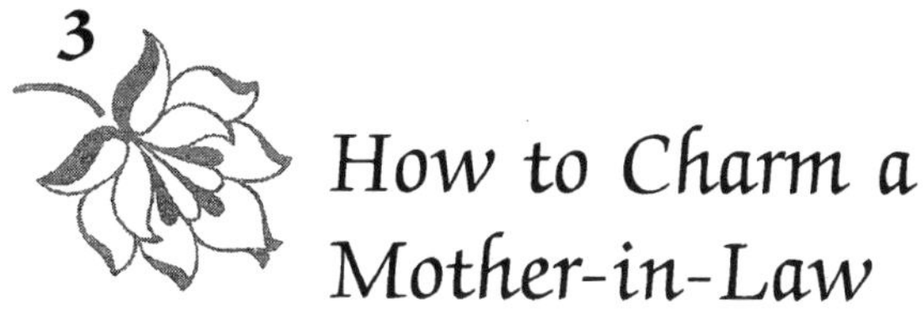

3 How to Charm a Mother-in-Law

My maternal grandparents were so happy that their eldest daughter would be spared the convent and was getting married, they couldn't have cared less that she was marrying a Chinese man. My grandfather had been convinced for years that she would marry a "foreigner" anyway, since she'd spent so much time in Mexico, studying art there, sending postcards from cities whose names were impossible to pronounce, learning to speak "those Mexicans' foreign language." My father even looked like a Mexican in my grandfather's eyes. He wasn't surprised at all by his daughter's choice.

My paternal grandmother, however, was shocked to discover that her son, her first-born, the one who was supposed to be closest to her, had found a bride without her expert matchmaking skills. She didn't care that my mother was not Chinese, but when she discovered that she was Catholic, Nai-nai's heart was nearly broken. The American missionaries in China had told her all about the papists. They weren't real Christians, they'd explained to my grandmother ever since she was a little girl. They were *Tianzhu jiao,* the Church of Heaven, not *Jidu jiao,* the Church of Jesus, as the terms had been translated into Chinese. Thus Catholics were, without a doubt, infidels. How could a son of hers possibly marry such a woman!

As my mother went about planning the wedding of her dreams—an elegant Grecian-style gown (nothing pouffy and lacy for her), the embossed announcements, the four-tier cake—my father told her nothing of the many negotiations he was undertaking with his mother. Soon he began to lose weight. Even in his sleep, he imagined his mother at his wedding, behaving as she did at the wedding ceremonies of those couples she had introduced, that is to say, like a matchmaker, the ultimate guest of honor, the mother of the bride and groom and their godparents rolled into one formidable presence who expected to be thanked. Not just thanked, but honored. Not just honored, but obeyed. Only it would be worse, much worse in this case, because my father was her first-born son, and she would expect to be honored in a dramatic and appropriately imperial manner. And secretly, deep in the most paranoid chamber of his heart, he worried that his mother might try to stop his marriage. She would be alarmed at how very Catholic the ceremony was. He had written to her, explaining that a Baptist minister would be present (just as she had requested), but he'd been vague about the details. If she saw, in fact, how little the Baptist had to do, perhaps she might even denounce them all dramatically. She was, after all, very religious, deeply Protestant, and utterly confident about the rightness of her views.

My father's clothes hung on his skeletal frame. He grew more and more nervous, jumping at little sounds like dogs barking in the distance, the echo of a bird's cry, crickets thrumming at night. He sweated profusely. One evening, he came to take my mother to a film and nearly fainted in her living room. She had to help him to the sofa, her arms wrapped firmly around his arm.

"What's wrong, Winberg?" she exclaimed in alarm. "Are you ill?"

And then he explained that they would have to get married immediately. He couldn't wait until May, he said. He wouldn't last until then. He may even have kissed her dramatically, passionately, as a sign of his desperate love.

My mother would have none of it. "I've waited thirty-two years for my wedding," she said firmly. "You can wait a few months more."

My father assented that evening, but he continued to grow thinner. He was wasting away before her eyes, and he shook visibly when they went out to university functions together. Even her mother noticed. "Just marry him," she said. "The poor man's lovesick!"

Finally, my father confessed to my mother what was worrying him. He didn't want his wedding to be a spectacle, a debacle, an item for gossip and rumor, not in a town this small, not with his tenure on the line. And he didn't want anything to prevent them from marrying. Or rather, anyone. He was afraid.

About this time, my mother's father also began to experience health problems, but of a different sort. He was an alcoholic, he was drinking heavily, he was losing his tenuous grasp on propriety. Again. My grandmother complained to my mother in long, sobbing phone calls.

My mother decided they should go see the priest and ask for his advice. After all, Lent had just begun, and it was impossible, as far as she knew, to get married during the six-week season of penitence that preceded Easter. If they could make it all the way to Easter Sunday in April, she didn't see why they couldn't hold out until May, as planned, but she knew the Lord worked in mysterious ways, and she would let the priest offer his opinion on the matter.

To her great surprise, the monsignor declared that hurrying the marriage would be no problem at all. He even knew of a way to get around the Lent problem. They could get married on St. Patrick's Day, which would certainly be appropriate given my mother's Irish roots. A saint's day, he explained, was a feast day according to the church, and was meant to be celebrated. Just because poor Saint Patrick's feast day fell in the middle of Lent, that didn't mean the Lord had intended that Patrick should be slighted. A wedding would be a fine way of honoring the saint.

And so my parents were married a few weeks later, on St. Patrick's Day. My mother wore an off-the-rack celadon-colored silk suit with a Jackie Kennedy–style pillbox hat instead of a veil. The elegant column of a wedding dress she had ordered had not come in on time. It was too late to change the wedding announcements, so she tossed them away. There was no cake, but to be truthful, neither of my parents was particularly fond of sweets. Ye-ye and Nai-nai did not have time to buy tickets to fly in from the coast for their first son's wedding. Thus the ceremony was small, religious, and spare. My mother persuaded a friend, a news photographer whom she had trained when she was director of the university's news bureau, to take the pictures. Because he was used to working with newspapers, all seven photographs of the service were in black and white.

My mother's wedding was nothing like the one she had planned, but later she agreed that it had turned out better that way. Her wedding was elegant and original. It fit my parents' style quite well.

That summer, my parents took their official honeymoon to New York City. My father was worried about his mother's reaction upon meeting his new bride for the first time, and he regaled my mother with terrible stories about his mother's temper, her long-standing blood feuds, her unforgiving nature. In fact, he worked himself up into quite a nervous lather, and when they arrived at my grandparents' apartment on West 71st Street, he was so wound up with worry that he immediately picked a fight with his mother without even thinking.

Before the introductions, before the family banquets welcoming the new bride into the family, before the group trip to Niagara Falls, the fighting began.

"You still have that couch!" my father exclaimed the moment he got in the door and saw the sheet-covered monstrosity listing against the wall. "You've had that couch for twelve years! It wasn't even new when you bought it. It's terrible, terrible!" He sat down upon it just to hear its springs squeak. "You should throw it away." He gestured to his brothers. "Come on, help me. Let's get rid of this thing. Help me put it on the curb!"

He couldn't stop himself. It was as though he were possessed. Once his mouth opened, he couldn't stop denigrating the couch.

"It's our couch! It's fine!" Nai-nai exclaimed in alarm. She threw up both hands to keep her sons from moving it. She scurried over and sat on one end and gestured for Ye-ye to follow suit. "You can't take my couch!"

Now my father felt even worse. "It's a terrible couch!"

"It's perfectly fine!"

He cast aside one edge of the sheet, revealing the stained, cigarette-burned brocade beneath. "Look at it!" He poked at one cushion and stuffing popped up through a particularly threadbare section of the upholstery.

They argued in Chinese and English, mixing phrases until they had created an entirely new language. My mother could make out very little of what they said, but she understood the essential details: her husband's red, embarrassed face as he waved frantically at the offending sofa, her mother-in-law's equally unhappy expression as she sat with her arms folded across her chest while sinking deeply into the moth-eaten cushions. My mother looked around the apartment quickly: it was filled with antiques and books and old furniture, balls of twine, a bowl of twist-ties that could be reused some day, a vial of denture cream on the end of a bookshelf, an armchair with the plastic still on the cushion, a pile of old Chinese newspapers in the kitchen, napkins nicked from the McDonald's on the corner. It was the apartment of a woman who had lived through a war and who wasn't going to throw anything away ever again. It reminded my mother immediately of her own family's home. Her mother had raised eight children and survived the Great Depression with just such thrift. Her mother was the kind of woman who would reuse paper cups and paper plates, washing them after a meal and stacking them in her cupboards. Even after they started to leak, she'd insist you drink quickly with a finger pressed to the hole rather than throw the damn thing away. My mother understood, all right.

"Actually, Winberg, I think it's a lovely couch. What good structure. They don't make couches like this anymore."

"It's terrible!" my father exclaimed.

"Let's go out now and see the sights," my mother suggested. "I've never seen New York before. Didn't you say we were going to Rockefeller Center?"

Ye-ye and my uncles seconded this motion, and my father was finally able to leave the apartment, although he still muttered to himself in the elevator and on the sidewalk below, "That couch, that couch, I can't believe she still has that ugly couch!"

Later that week, as my father took my mother shopping around the city, she found a fabric outlet store in the garment district and bought a bolt of beautiful red brocade. Perhaps the offending couch could be resuscitated, she explained to my father. Just trust me, she said. She had an idea.

That afternoon, after the many-course Chinese banquet my grandfather had prepared for everyone, my father's family all lay down to take a nap. Nai-nai and Ye-ye retired to their rooms, my uncles stretched out in easy chairs, even my father curled up in a chair to sleep. The apartment was stuffy and warm—it was a muggy day in the city and the tiny air conditioner in the window barely made a dent in the heat—and they all fell asleep fairly quickly. My mother was not accustomed to this family habit: certainly my father didn't take such naps when he was home in Redlands, but he snored contentedly, returning to the habits of his youth now that he was back with his family.

While they slept, my mother decided to reupholster her mother-in-law's sofa. My mother had never actually reupholstered any furniture before, but she knew how to sew and figured she'd give it a try. She didn't ask anyone first, she didn't say what she was going to do; she simply took the stuffing she'd purchased out of its bag and refilled the cushions and the back and arms until they looked almost normal. Then she laid the fabric across the sofa, pinning and tacking and poking and prodding until it stayed in place, and finally began to sew. The red brocade was a chinoiserie print, with an ornate peony motif and a rich strand of gold thread running vertically every six inches or so. My mother thought it complemented the apartment's many colors quite well and contrasted rather nicely with the scroll of black ink calligraphy on the wall behind the sofa.

By the time my grandfather woke, roughly an hour later, he was shocked to discover his daughter-in-law kneeling before a bright red sofa. My uncles and father more so. They had to admit, the sofa looked stunning, but they had no idea how Nai-nai would react. They'd never actually dared to touch her precious couch.

At last, Nai-nai shuffled into the living room, rubbing her eyes and stifling a yawn. Her eyes widened when she saw the sofa.

Far from being angry, she beamed. "You see!" she exclaimed, pointing at my father's nose. "I always told you it was a perfectly good couch!"

When my mother was finished, Nai-nai was so pleased that she made my grandfather put a brand-new sheet atop the pretty couch to keep it nice. She didn't even want the old sheet touching it.

My mother tried to persuade her to leave the sheet off. "I can always reupholster it again," she said, but my grandmother wouldn't hear of it.

"No, too much work for you." And Nai-nai tucked the sheet in gently around the armrests.

My *grandmother's relationship* to her daughter-in-law was thus sealed for all time. Nai-nai couldn't believe her good luck. It was she who insisted now that she and my grandfather pay for the family's "honeymoon trip" to Niagara Falls. Her fears that her son was marrying a papist, someone she had not specifically picked for him, a woman whose family she'd never met, all vanished. For years to come, she'd tell this story to all her friends, to the old ladies in her senior center, to the women at the Chinese bakery, to anyone who'd listen. How her daughter-in-law had sided with her in an argument and not with her husband!

"She agreed with me!" she nodded proudly. "It's a good couch! She doesn't waste money, this daughter-in-law. She made it look like new!"

And the blue-haired ladies at the senior center agreed, clicking their tongues against their dentures, whistling through puckered lips. A daughter-in-law who appreciates her mother-in-law's wisdom, now that's a girl worth her weight in gold!

4

California Dreamin'

Naturally there were some people who warned my parents that they should not have children. My parents married in 1966, not long after the 1964 Civil Rights Act banned the antimiscegenation laws of old and a year before the Supreme Court confirmed the ban in the aptly titled case of *Loving v. Virginia.* There were still many fears and prejudices about "mixed marriages," and even the most educated people could say the dumbest things. One nurse acted as though my parents were two entirely different species, an amphibian and a bird, a mammal and a fish, when she heard that my mother was pregnant. "But what will the child be?"

"Beautiful," my father said with confidence.

Thus in June 1967 I was born, a member of the first generation of Americans who were legally biracial. We could not be called bastards in any state's records, we could not have our parentage denied: we were legal. Then, in the summer of 1968, my brother was born. We both had two eyes, two ears, a nose, a mouth, ten fingers and toes. Just beautiful, my father proclaimed, as predicted.

Fast forward to paradise.

It's late spring, the air redolent with the scent of honeysuckle and orange blossoms. The heat in Southern California is already intense.

Adults' voices float from the open windows of our house. Then laughter. I pass more mud to my brother. Our parents are having a party and we've been exiled to the backyard, where I have decided to paint all the trees brown, for revenge. Our dogs lie prone in the shade, their legs twitching as they run in their sleep. My brother, both hands plunged in the hole we have dug and filled with water, obediently mixes dirt and water with the intensity of a French pastry chef.

Spanish and English phrases fly from the windows like hummingbirds and hang in the still air. My mother's friends are visiting. They are artists, too, mostly from Mexico, where my mother went to school. Today I am *Carolina's* daughter.

My father is mixing drinks and telling anecdotes. I can hear his voice boom louder as he reaches the punch line. Explosive laughter.

"Come on." I nudge my brother, who has become absorbed in the movements of an earthworm. Obediently, he picks up his red plastic bucket of mud and follows me to the plum tree at the very back of the yard. We are naked except for our diapers and the coat of mud drying against our tan skin. I could be three or four, my brother a year younger.

Later the adults will spill from the house, drinks in hand, and laugh to see the way we have painted the trees. They will misunderstand my intentions.

"Look, Carolina's daughter wants to be an artist!" In Spanish and English they will laugh, all their bright, sharp teeth shining in the late afternoon sun.

My parents laugh as well, and my brother runs to them, dropping his bucket of mud. They bend, smiling, and my heart melts, forgiving them for their party, for excluding me, and then I'm running too, ready to be welcomed back into my parents' arms.

As a child in California, in the small town of Redlands where my parents had met and married and where I was born, my springs were Mexican. Our house was routinely brimming with my mother's artist friends, their works covered our walls; mixing with my father's Chinese scrolls were an assortment of saints in various unhappy postures, a burlap Madonna, a ceramic black sea of flying green fish. I remember in particular a long vertical painting composed of drops of paint forming a highly textured surface and no discernible image except for a giant gray eyeball at the top of a narrow white V. My parents hung it at the end of the hallway, where I felt that eyeball watching me wherever I went, even when I hid beneath the coffee table in the living room or behind the sofa or wrapped within the draperies. After my parents realized the source of my strange behavior, they moved the painting to the far corner of the living room beside the piano, and I stopped creeping throughout the house.

In the summer, however, our life became Chinese.

My father's parents came to visit every year, staying for several months at a time. They were allowed to take over our TV room and I was told not to disturb them there. But sometimes I peeked at them through the doorway and watched as my grandmother sat on the sofa bed in a cotton *qipao,* combing out her long gray braid, while my grandfather stirred at his dentures in a clear glass of water. The image of his teeth floating outside of his mouth frightened me, and once I must have gasped, because suddenly both Ye-ye and Nai-nai looked up and smiled at me, then gestured for me to come inside their room, raising their hands palm downward, wagging their fingers, but I ran away quickly.

There was only one Chinese restaurant in our town, Tang's Café, where the owners made stir-fry and burgers if you wanted them. Mr. Tang was always very happy to see our family and invited us over to his house. The Tangs had an enormous in-ground swimming pool that shimmered as blue as the sky. My parents wouldn't let me go near it because I didn't know how to swim yet, but their son, who was slightly older, was a showoff, abandoning me on the patio to jump cannonballs off the side, over and over, tucking his golden legs under his body as he plunged into the pool. Mr. Tang had had no formal education and worked very hard for his family, so that they would have all the material comforts an American life could provide. He even cleaned the family pool himself, rising early to vacuum the bits of leaves and insects that had blown in overnight, and he developed a deep tan from the sunlight reflecting off the water. Years after we'd moved away, we received a note from his wife. He'd fallen into the pool while cleaning it for the children and had drowned. He'd never learned to swim; when had he ever had the time? No one thought to look in the pool that morning; they all assumed he'd gone to work. When they finally found his body hours later, floating next to the leaf net, it was too late.

When my grandparents visited in the summer, Ye-ye liked to cook for us. He was intent upon discovering a way to use American ingredients to make Chinese dishes. He found a way to turn Pillsbury biscuits out of the canister into *bao-zi* dough that, when steamed with a filling, tasted almost Chinese, and he invented a sweet-and-sour sauce from ketchup, mustard, brown sugar, and soy sauce that was quite delicious on pork chops. But other experiments did not turn out so well. One year, when I was very little, he decided to prepare a pressed duck. Who knows where he managed to buy the bird, but he slit its throat and then hung the duck off the eaves of our house to let the blood drain out. He was convinced that the intense Southern California sunlight would act as a kind of oven and would dry out the meat, but after a day the carcass merely began to rot and my father had to cut it down and throw it away lest the neighbors think we were lunatics.

Perhaps it was that summer that my grandmother killed my mother's canary, a bird my father had bought her for their first anniversary and which they had named in a fit of whimsy "Tony Wong." Nai-nai was convinced that it was unhealthy for a bird to remain indoors all day. It was cruel, even, although Tony Wong's cage was near a window so that he could look out into our yard at the bougainvillea and the rosebushes and the flowering oleander shrub. In China, men liked to take their songbirds into the public parks and hang their cages in the trees while they gossiped or played chess or practiced tai chi. A bird needed fresh air, my grandmother insisted. When my mother refused to heed her advice, Nai-nai took matters into her own hands, and one night, after everyone else had gone to sleep, she rose in the moonlight and opened the window behind Tony Wong's cage so that the cool night breezes that blew in from the mountains could waft through his cage and bring him some happiness.

The next morning I found Tony Wong asleep with his head tucked tightly under his yellow wing. Even when I tapped on the bars of his cage, he did not wake and sing as usual. When my mother found him, she let out a shriek, which frightened me. I ran into the kitchen to hide under the table there. Soon my father and grandparents were gathered around her. She was crying. My father stuck his hand through the cage door and prodded Tong Wong with one finger, but he did not move from his perch. I knew from previous experience with my two goldfish what death was and what happened to creatures that died: my father flushed them down the toilet. I did not want to see poor Tony Wong suffer such a fate, and so I closed my eyes tightly and covered my ears with my hands until the cage was gone and it was safe for me to come out from under the table.

Because of these incidents with the duck and the canary, my grandparents took on an aura of both mystery and danger in my eyes, which I found enticing. They were nothing like the other old people I knew in our town, who were full of rules and admonitions, who constantly said things like "Don't run around" and "Don't speak until you're spoken to" and "Lower your voice in the house."

My grandparents shouted to each other quite loudly in Mandarin throughout the house. They laughed when I ran through the hall. They marveled at my ability to speak English with an American accent—as though they couldn't believe their own flesh and blood could achieve such a thing—and they never minded when I chattered nonstop in their presence. And best of all they smiled whenever they caught me peeking into their room. My disobedience was seen as a sign of great intelligence. My brother was still a toddler, just a baby who couldn't talk yet and who might cry unexpectedly, so at this point in my life, I was the favored first-born child.

When I discovered that my grandparents had no idea about rules, I was able to enlist their help in many endeavors. They let me come into their room and watch the television anytime I wanted. They fed me snacks between meals. They let me jump on the sofa bed when my parents weren't looking.

One of my earliest memories involves my grandfather. I would wake up well before my parents or brother, and normally would have to lie in my crib waiting for my mother to wake up before I could do anything. But when my grandparents were visiting, I needed only to whisper his name, "Ye-ye, Ye-ye, Ye-ye," over and over like a prayer, and he would appear at my bedside. I would raise my arms into the air and he would pull me from the crib. I told him to get me dressed, and he did. Then I told him to get my stroller, and he did that as well. He put on his long gray Chinese gown that he liked to wear in those days—later, in New York, I would see him only in suits, but in the heat of California he reverted to his Chinese clothing—and he would push me in my stroller down the sidewalk until we reached our neighbor's house, where the little girl I liked to play with lived. Then I would tell Ye-ye to drop me off and go home. Sometimes my mother would catch us as we departed, and she would come running after us in her robe, saying it was too early for visiting my friend, and make us come home. But the next morning, if she was still asleep, I could always persuade Ye-ye to take me out again.

Once, when I was older, Nai-nai walked with me in our backyard and pointed to the leaves of our mulberry tree. She pulled a branch down and held my hand to the leaf, which was only slightly longer than my fingers.

"What big hands you have," she said. "As big as this leaf."

I nodded proudly.

"We had trees like this in China," she told me then. "My mother fed the leaves to her worms to make silk."

Then she let the branch spring back, the leaves fluttering in the breeze.

I had no idea what she meant. Feeding leaves to worms. Making silk. Her having a mother. My grandparents were the oldest people on earth. They had always been old, they were older than my parents, even. They were like the sky. Like the stars. I couldn't imagine Nai-nai having such a thing as a mother. Why would she need one? But I kept these thoughts to myself, puzzling over them silently. I had no idea how to put them into words.

After my grandfather's second heart attack, Ye-ye and Nai-nai stopped coming to spend the summer with us.

Sometimes we would visit my mother's parents, who lived in our town, but my grandfather was never feeling well. I did not understand that he was a recovering alcoholic or that he had emphysema and was in a lot of pain. Instead I thought of him as a grumpy man, a man who rarely smiled, the kind of old person who was full of rules. My grandmother was always happy to see us, but she seemed tired, she had my grandfather to look after day and night, and we never visited for very long.

By this time I had started kindergarten, and my social life expanded beyond my family. I had a boyfriend named Lupe who rode the bus to my school from the Mexican side of town. He liked to call me on the phone, which infuriated my father, who forbade me to call him back. I had another boyfriend named Scott, whose big sister once dragged him from our house by the ankles, crying and screaming, after he'd followed me home after school to show me his collection of dried-apple dolls, which turned out to belong to his sister. I had a best friend named Kathleen, whose parents were Mexican artists and who came to our house and spoke Spanish with my mother while we played in the backyard. Kathleen only had an older brother, a teenager, who was moody and unfriendly, whereas my little brother was obedient and cheerful and would always play with us, even when that meant we dressed him up as Peter Pan in a green hat and shorts with leaves stuffed in the waistband so that we could be Tiger Lily and Wendy and pretend to fly through our yard with our arms outstretched.

When I was young, I never worried about my parents, what they were thinking or feeling. It was a surprise, then, when they began to argue the year that I turned five, when pottery began to be thrown against walls and plates smashed on the floor.

They argued in dramatic ways just as they showed their affection in dramatic ways, with giant bouquets from my father suddenly appearing on the kitchen table or a new painting by my mother appearing on a wall—a scene from their honeymoon in New York, my parents transformed into lovers kissing on a park bench, or something more abstract, like the giant red and blue yin-yang circle filled with flowers, the tapestry made of appliquéd vermilion blossoms, the canvas radiating with the hot white sun.

Their moods made no more sense to me than the rising of the sun or the appearance of stars at night. They simply existed.

It was only later that I would begin to understand.

My *father wanted to leave California.*

He would later admit, decades and decades later, that he had had everything a man could have wanted in our town: a beautiful wife and two children, a girl and a boy, a matched set, and the kind of small-town happiness such a confluence of good luck suggested. We lived in a small house in a good neighborhood, a chain-link fence to keep the children from running out into the street, two dogs to play with the children. We had our own orange grove in the backyard as well as a plum tree, a giant mulberry, pink bougainvillea vines that covered an entire wall of the house, a small plot of bamboo, a jade plant, and enough lawn to keep him busy with the mower every three weeks. He joined the Lions Club and the Knights of Columbus. Our neighbors all knew our names and invited us to backyard barbecues. On weekends we climbed into the large Buick Electra Limited that he'd purchased from one of his students after he graduated—an Arabian prince in fact; who else could have afforded such a car when it was new?—and we headed off for a day in the nearby Big Bear mountains or else to the shore near San Diego. The weather was always beautiful, the summers hot but never humid, the winters just chilly enough for a sweater but never cold. It snowed exactly once in the eight years my father spent in California, a brief freak snow shower that caused my brother and me to run out the front door in delight, hands outstretched to cup a snowflake in our palms. The snow melted even before touching the ground.

Were we not living the very American Dream that my grandparents had fought so hard for us to have? Had they not struggled for years in China to keep their children alive during the wars just so that someday their grandchildren might live this sort of idyllic life? Or was our life even better than they could have imagined in those days, while the family huddled in air raid shelters as Japanese bombers strafed their city, while my grandparents waited in long lines for the meager rations of rice-flour buns that were allotted each family by the government, while they prayed aloud at night to an invisible God to save us, to spare us, to protect us so that another generation might live and prosper sometime in the distant and difficult-to-imagine future?

Our life in California was in many ways perfect. Yet my father was not happy in the sleepy town of Redlands, where the air always smelled of orange blossoms, where the horizon was dotted with palm and eucalyptus trees instead of skyscrapers, where one had to drive sixty-five miles to L.A.'s Chinatown to get a decent Chinese meal. Here he'd met his wife, my mother; he had sired his children, my brother and me; he had achieved tenure.

But my father missed the energy of New York, the ambition, the greed, the nervous neurotic need to see and be seen, to walk in the throbbing humming pulsing center of the world, striving and thriving, cursing and cussing, seeking, searching, being. He wanted to feel the rush of adrenaline that he got every time he walked down the crowded sidewalks. He wanted to know that his work was important, that he was influential, that he was fulfilling his destiny in the greatest city the world had ever known.

In Redlands, his students were polite, but for the most part they were not impassioned. They were living in the paradise known as Southern California in a small, affluent, predominantly upper-middle-class town. There were no hippies holding love-ins, no draft dodgers burning their draft cards in the street, no antiwar protesters, no civil rights marchers, no anarchists, no activists. Everyone was far too polite for that.

It might have been the perfect life for some, but my father felt he was missing out on something more important. A sense of history.

Destiny. Or maybe just ego. When you're young and ambitious, these things can be difficult to tell apart.

He applied for new jobs, anything that would take him back to New York. And when he received the job offer from CCNY, he accepted it immediately, even though my mother cried, my brother and I cried, and we were pitiful to behold. We did not want to leave our home, but my father could not imagine staying any longer.

There's a Chinese curse: May all your wishes come true. There's an American saying: Hindsight's always twenty-twenty.

What can I say now? At the time, we paid no attention to pithy aphorisms. My father had the more pressing issue of his destiny to attend to.

Thus, in 1973, he became chairman of the newly created Department of Asian Studies at the City College of New York and returned to the city of his dreams.

Little did he realize how much New York had changed in the eight years he'd been away.

The Revolution was under way.

5 The Banana

His first day on campus, as he walked from the parking lot to his office in the series of Gothic-style stone buildings that housed the newly created ethnic studies departments, my father thought to himself how the architecture recalled a medieval European monastery more than an urban college. Students, perhaps feeling the same sentiment, had spray-painted the walls with graffiti: Fuck the Man! Get Whitey! The Revolution is NOW! Students marched along the green carrying placards and banners: "End the war in Vietnam!" "Don't Kill Our Yellow Brothers!" They looked nothing like the students back in Redlands. Every shade of the human race was represented. They wore their hair long or in thick Afros. They dressed in fringed vests, bell-bottoms, T-shirts with various slogans hand-printed across the fronts and backs. They wore buttons proclaiming their political alliances: Black Power, Yellow Power, Puerto Rican Independence, Free Love. My father was amused to see several Chinese students, obviously American-raised by their dress and comportment, wearing Mao buttons and even a T-shirt proclaiming allegiance with the Red Guards. Mao had launched the Great Proletarian Cultural Revolution in 1966, shutting down the universities for a year and then reopening them in a highly restricted manner based on a class system that penalized educated families while sending students and intellectuals to the countryside "to learn from the peasants." It was funny to think that such an urban population as City College's Chinese students would find inspiration in an agrarian revolutionary movement that denigrated university education, and my father may even have laughed to himself. Later, of course, the wannabe Red Guards would seem less funny, but at the time he was too excited about being back in the city to worry about the implications of their politics.

He knew that in 1969 many radical students had taken over buildings, demonstrated, fought, set fires, and otherwise demanded an increase in minority enrollment. At that time, less than 5 percent of the student body at CCNY were ethnic minorities, yet minorities constituted 60 percent of New York's public school students. Many professors felt the students had a point. The college obviously wasn't representative of the city anymore, yet no one could agree on a remedy.

City College had once been the pride of New York's public education system, an affordable college for the children of the city's working immigrant population. Founded in 1847, the school offered a good education with free tuition. In the early days, the students were mostly European immigrants. The school had earned a good reputation despite the fact that its students didn't come from money, and its alumni included Jonas Salk, the inventor of the polio vaccine; eight Nobel laureates; writers Irving Kristol, Bernard Malamud, and Alfred Kazin; social scientist Seymour Martin Lipset; and the *New York Times* executive editor and columnist A. M. Rosenthal.[1]

By the 1960s, however, the ethnic makeup of the city had changed. The Jewish immigrants of an earlier era had prospered and moved on, and Harlem was now mostly black and Latino. The city's public schools had large numbers of Chinese students as well, and they wanted to come to City College but often could not meet the college's stringent and European-centered entrance requirements. These students were the sons and daughters of Chinatown's working poor. Their parents had not come on scholarships to attend American universities as my father's had, but rather had worked for low wages in

[1]James Traub, *City on a Hill: Testing the American Dream at City College* (New York: Addison-Wesley, 1995), 10; and Theodore L. Gross, *Academic Turmoil: The Reality and Promise of Open Education* (Garden City, N.Y.: Anchor Press/Doubleday, 1980), 8.

laundries and restaurants and other small businesses, facing discrimination and violence throughout their lives. Their children had gone to overcrowded public schools and had struggled as bilingual students in an English-only curriculum with tired, overworked teachers who had ill prepared them for higher education.

In 1970 the New York Board of Education had tried to adapt to the changing needs of the city's population by adopting an "open admissions" policy, meaning essentially that anyone who had graduated in the top half of their New York high school could now enroll in classes at the college. This proved to be a highly controversial decision. Overnight the student body changed. Although 60 percent of the students who benefited were white, they were the children of more recent immigrants—Greek, Italian, Ukrainian, Slavic, Irish—and there were fewer Jewish students than in the past. And African American students now accounted for 20.5 percent of the student body, Puerto Ricans for 6.6 percent, and Asian (mostly Chinese American) for 5.2 percent.[2]

The Asian students soon rallied together and joined forces with the blacks and Latinos to press for curriculum changes. They wanted courses that reflected the fact that other, non-European minorities had contributed to the building of America. By 1971 they were calling for the creation of new departments, and by 1973 my father had became the first chair of the newly created Department of Asian Studies.

Cantonese and Spanish were offered now in addition to French and German. Top scholars of color congregated at the college. The writers Alex Haley and Elie Wiesel had offices down the hall from my father. As chair of the Asian Studies Department, my father was able to recruit and hire top scholars in Chinese studies—people like Priscilla Ching Chung, a Ph.D. from Penn who specialized in the history of Chinese women. Artists like Danny Yung, who would later form the internationally renowned Hong Kong dance troupe Zuni Icosohedron, taught on campus. Professors like Diana Kao encouraged students to undertake oral histories in Chinatown so that their parents' and grandparents' history would not be lost. Sociologist Betty Lee Sung was almost single-handedly rewriting Chinese American

[2] Gross, *Academic Turmoil,* 15–16.

history with her books on gold miners and railroad workers. Historian T. K. Tong enabled students to study the glories and tribulations of the history of China. My father himself formed the Asian American Assembly for Policy Research, the first such political advocacy group for Asian Americans, and received grants from the Henry Luce Foundation. These were heady times, and my father and his colleagues were convinced that they could reshape the world.

Naturally, there were some in the administration who opposed the formation of separate ethnic studies departments, upper-division courses changed to remedial courses needed to bring the open-admission students up to speed academically, and the changing curricular demands of the students. Sometimes the faculty senate meetings were highly contentious, with much shouting and table thumping as everyone competed for scarce resources. Okay, not sometimes—*always.* New York was in the midst of a worsening recession, and the budget woes came at a time when admissions were increasing rapidly.

There were other problems beyond academic concerns. Big problems. For example, some radicals vowed they would bring the Cultural Revolution to New York, and they carried their own version of the Little Red Book in their hands as they paraded across the campus. They disrupted classes, shouting down the professors. They marched through the hallways. They wanted revolution, all right, although it was never very clear what kind of revolution that would be. It was an amorphous, all-encompassing revolution that would rectify the discrimination of the past, make up for their parents' poverty, for the long hours their mothers and fathers had worked in restaurants and laundries and sweatshops. They would oppose the System with a capital "S" that had led to the war in Vietnam, to the draft that unfairly fell most heavily on the children of the poor and minorities, and to the overcrowded, inadequate public schools.

Some of these Chinese radicals teamed up with students from other ethnic groups. Many had no affiliation with the campus and weren't even students. They began to demand a revolutionary overthrow of the administration; they were antiwhite, anti-Semitic, forgetting that members of other ethnic and religious groups had also faced discrimination in their own lives. Their disruptive theatrics prevented normal teaching and learning. They threatened professors and students who didn't agree with them.

I remember the day my father took to wearing casual clothes to work, a black turtleneck and a plaid sports jacket. I'd never seen my father leave for work without a suit and tie. He'd always dressed in the modern equivalent of his father's suits. In China, my grandfather had worn a scholar's robe made of blue silk. Later, in Taiwan, he adopted American-style suits, a trend he continued in the United States. I'd seen the family pictures, small black-and-white photos in a jumbled family album. There was Ye-ye in his classrooms at the New School and Hunter College, demonstrating the art of calligraphy. His suit was a little large for his frame—his bone structure was so small by American standards that he had to buy his shoes in the children's department—but he never left for work without his three-piece suit, a tie knotted at his throat, his black children's dress shoes carefully polished. Now my father was dressing like Starsky and Hutch doing undercover police work. I thought it was cool and told him so, but he merely nodded grimly, as my mother pecked him on the cheek and wished him good luck.

But my father's undercover look fooled no one, especially not his students. He was still branded a square, a suit, a counterrevolutionary. Even though he had been born and raised in China, because he had a Ph.D. and his family members were all educated, he was accused of being a member of the White Establishment—in other words a "banana," yellow on the outside, white on the inside.

The irony, of course, was that no Chinese person from China would ever have guessed that it was un-Chinese to be educated. It was in fact the goal of generation after generation of Chinese, since the civil service exam system that promised wealth, power, and prestige to any family whose son could pass the miserable, three-day affair had first been initiated in the Han Dynasty sometime in the second century C.E.

Then things got worse. Faculty in the department complained to him that some radicals had threatened them if they didn't receive

A's—even when they didn't attend class. These students claimed they should be given credit for experience on the streets. Radical groups began to harass white faculty from other departments who came to visit Asian Studies faculty. I heard my father talking to my mother in the kitchen late at night, when I was supposed to be asleep in bed. I sat on the staircase, my face pressed between the bars of the banister, while my father recounted how a very nice Russian history professor had been locked into the bathroom that day, the students quickly nailing two-by-fours across the door so that he couldn't leave. Finally someone heard his frantic pounding and managed to pry him free. The radicals didn't want him visiting the Asian Studies Department because he was a white man. Yet he had spent many years of his youth living in Shanghai, where his family had fled after the Russian Revolution of 1917.

My father stayed up later and later after he came home from work. He took to drinking a Scotch, first one, then two. I could hear the tinkling of the ice from my bedroom.

Thugs and criminals were hiding amid the students, he told my mother. They were taking advantage of the chaos and stealing from the offices.

It became harder and harder to teach. My father was afraid that some of the agitators might become violent—they threatened to do so if the professors didn't listen to their demands, which changed from week to week. Sometimes they wanted popular teachers to be granted tenure immediately, even if they didn't have their doctorates in hand. They wanted other professors fired. They wanted Asian Studies to merge with Black Studies so that with their combined numbers, they could "take back City College from the Jews."

My father stayed at work later and later, meeting with other faculty members, trying to sort out what to do. He came home well past midnight. My mother waited up for him, while I was supposed to be asleep like my brother.

"We should leave." I heard my mother's voice one night, firm, determined. "We can go back to California."

I heard the ice tinkling in my father's glass of Scotch, but from my perch on the stairs I couldn't hear his reply.

My brother and I took to sleeping with my mother in my parents' king-size bed. We couldn't sleep in our separate rooms, knowing that he was still in the city. My mother read us books, and when she was too nervous to read, she told us stories about her childhood, growing up on a farm, until at last we heard my father's Buick pull into the driveway and we could relax for another night.

6

The Banana's Revenge

And then, suddenly, things seemed to take a turn for the better.

At one of my father's NYU night classes he met a young redheaded law student named Nancy Oxfeld who had elected to take one of his classes on China. She had enjoyed his lectures and thought he'd get along with her father—so she arranged for them to meet. It turned out that her father, Emil, was also a lawyer, a founding member of the ACLU in New Jersey. My father and Emil hit it off immediately. Emil was unflappable. Nothing my father told him shook his faith in the world. Once I watched him toss his head back and roar with laughter while my father told him stories about his fractious days at CCNY. His laughter had a calming effect on my father, and soon I no longer heard the tinkling of ice before he came to bed. He no longer had to whisper to my mother in the kitchen. He could laugh with Emil on the phone.

As the phone happened to be in my room, rather than in my parents' (a design quirk of our house), I heard many of his late-night conversations, as my father shouted and laughed into the phone while I lay with a pillow over my head, pretending I was asleep.

My father was most concerned about the potential for violence on the campus. At one point the dean actually was assigned armed guards to protect him in his office. But Emil quickly thought of some solutions. He knew many radical speakers—more radical even than the ones the students had been able to bring to campus—and he said he'd help my father bring them to his classes. This would help to bring down my father's square quotient and gain the students' trust. Then he offered advice about avoiding confrontation.

"Conciliation," my father repeated into the phone. "Right, right. Conciliation, not confrontation."

And then Emil must have said something funny because my father started laughing again, bending over and holding his hand to his thigh as though to keep himself from falling over with mirth.

The turning point came when my father discovered that some radical agitators were trying to organize the students to demonstrate against him at an upcoming faculty senate meeting. The president would be there and they wanted to show him that my father had no support, that *they*, not he, should choose the chairman of the department. My father was so worried he couldn't eat breakfast that morning. Instead he paced in the kitchen, wiping his sweaty palms against the knees of his polyester slacks.

"If these radicals show up, the president will fire me. He'll say I've lost control of the department." He paced between the stove and the avocado-colored refrigerator.

"Eat your breakfast," my mother commanded and forced a slice of toast into his hand.

"I'll lose my job," my father said, then nibbled the toast. He tried to say something more but started to choke. My mother patted him on the back calmly and handed him a cup of coffee.

"Don't worry," she said. "God will protect you."

My father's face was bright red now, whether from panic or the choking episode I couldn't tell, and I stopped eating my Froot Loops to stare at him in alarm. My mother patted him on the back some more, and slowly his face returned to a more human color.

"Just remember what Emil told you," she said. "And if all else fails, remember to laugh."

As my father would later recount, not once or twice but at least thirty times before I gave up counting and plugged my ears just to avoid hearing the story again, Emil's words were indeed prophetic.

As the faculty senate convened, my father looked up at the dais and saw the dean and the president sitting side by side. They looked tired, stressed out. They looked terrible. They looked exactly as my father imagined himself.

And then, with horror, he could see them pouring into the room—demonstrators! My father recognized clearly the angry faces of the radicals, many of whom had in fact already left City College and were no longer students, as well as the befuddled faces of the young people they'd persuaded to come to this so-called "rally." Many of the young people weren't students either, but because they were Chinese Americans, the radicals thought they could pass them off as students from the Asian Studies Department. It was true that most students in the department were Chinese, but my father was insulted that these radicals would assume that he wouldn't be able to tell total strangers from his students. That he, of all people, would think all Chinese looked alike.

And as he grew angrier and angrier, he could feel the heat rising to his face, and he knew from past experience that he must be growing quite red and hideous-looking. He glanced over at the dean, who was looking at him now with genuine concern at seeing one of his chairpersons turning such a color, but my father hardly cared, and he turned away, thinking, "If these hoodlums want a fight, I'll give them a fight!"

But then he could hear Emil's voice in his ear. "Remember, no direct confrontations. Conciliation, conciliation," the voice urged.

And then my father could hear Emil's laugh. As clearly as though his friend were standing there next to him. Emil was laughing at this absurd situation, where a room was filling up with strangers, waiters and waitresses from Chinatown, shop girls and busboys, all to play-act as students for an afternoon and denounce Chai, the Square Chair. My father's heart began to calm. He was sweating less profusely. He was no longer angry or even afraid. He, too, felt like laughing.

And as agitators continued to file into the room, he suddenly jumped up on top of his chair, to the surprise of his colleagues seated next to him.

"Down with Chai!" he shouted, raising a fist in the air. "Down with Chai! Down with Chai!"

The young people in the room looked startled. They weren't sure what to do. Some of them began to chant along, "Down with Chai! Down with Chai!" Obviously, they assumed he was one of the radical group organizers. He was a Chinese man shouting, after all. And so they did exactly as my father did. When he waved one fist, they waved one fist. When he began waving both fists, they followed suit.

Now the real organizers began to get angry. My father recognized one of them in the audience, a young woman who called herself "Spring Moon" and who had vowed personally to bring Mao's revolution to City College. She frowned now and with furrowed brows began running among the Chinatown kids, trying to get them to lower their arms and quit shouting. This wasn't their cue, she seemed to be saying. *Don't you know, that man is Chai! You shouldn't be listening to him!*

Now, while half the room was chanting, the other half was being told to shush. My father's colleagues in the department, the dean, and the president were in stitches. Finally, in a fit of frustration, Spring Moon gave up and waved her followers outside. Soon the room quieted down and everyone was able to conduct business in relative peace.

"I looked over at the president, and I knew at that moment, I had saved my job," my father proclaimed proudly. "He felt I could handle the situation all right. That Chai really knows how to keep control."

My father was telling the story of his triumph for what seemed like the millionth time, but everyone at our Thanksgiving table burst into laughter. We'd invited the Oxfelds over for dinner and Emil had wanted to hear the tale "one more time." I'd groaned inwardly, but there was no stopping it. I was especially peeved because I'd had a secret plan to take on the Oxfeld daughters, Nancy and Ellen, at ping-pong. They were college girls, and my brother and I were only in elementary school, but I knew for a fact that they didn't have a ping-pong table at home, and so I figured we'd have the advantage. I was looking forward to beating them at doubles, but unfortunately my mother had decided to use the ping-pong table as our Thanksgiving table. She'd promised we could clear it off after dinner, but now none of the adults wanted to move. My mother and Edith—Nancy and Ellen's mother—were deep in conversation the way only adults seemed to be capable of, forgetting to move, ignoring all the fun things that one could do as they talked on and on and on. They sat planted around the ping-pong table, still laden with dishes and carved turkey, gravy boats and dirty plates, as though they could sit like this forever.

And then, to my horror, Emil said it, his ruddy face breaking into a smile. "Win, tell it again. Tell me again what happened."

I looked at my brother then and he shrugged. We knew it was hopeless. There'd be no ping-pong for us this Thanksgiving.

What I didn't know then was that soon we'd be moving. My father would accept the job in South Dakota, all in the hope of getting away from the stress of the city, seeking a more bucolic life, the kind that existed in the movies (but not in real life), and we wouldn't see the Oxfelds again for years, nor would my father be able to laugh so easily, not like this, not with his friend.

7 Autumn in the Country

I can always date our family photos by the color of my mother's hair.

When I was six, my mother dyed her hair a severe onyx black and wore it pulled back in tight chignons. The effect was very chic, but looking back at family photos, I can now see the stress in her face, her skin too pale beneath her inky hair. All her paintings from this era reflect a similar aesthetic: dark blues and violets, rigid vertical lines, flowers with petals as sharp as metal, portraits of people who do not smile but stare tensely out of the corner of their eyes.

That year, 1973, we had moved from my mother's hometown of Redlands, California, to northern New Jersey, so that my father the New Yorker could accept the job at City College. (This is how my brother and I used to think of our parents: as the New Yorker and the California Artist, never as the Chinese Professor and the White American, or later—as kids in school would put it—the Chink and the Floozy.) After decades of Southern California sunshine, however, my mother couldn't get used to the overcast skies, the damp winters, the humid summers. All her contacts were in California, and now, for the first time in her life, she did not have a professional career. She taught weekend enrichment classes for children and edited and typed my father's books, but this was hardly satisfying. What's more, we were living in the suburbs, in a working-class bedroom community, whereas she was used to living in a university town where there were cultural events, concerts, and art exhibits every week.

Before my brother and I were born, when my parents were newly married, my mother had had auburn hair, which photographed a beautiful cherry-wood red in sunlight. After we were born she began dying her hair a darker brown so that we would all match. She also owned a small collection of wigs, bobs and pin curls, frosted blonde locks and long, dark, Cher-like tresses. Such things seemed quite normal in that era. My brother and I used to try them on for fun.

Finally, in our fifth year in New Jersey, when I was eleven, my mother decided to go for a radical change and had her hairdresser lop off her shoulder-length hair and perm what was left. She stopped setting her hair in rollers, she no longer teased it into tall buns atop her head. Instead it was all scrunch and go. She began working more and more outside the home, teaching night classes at a nearby college, serving on the environmental board for our town, offering art enrichment classes for adults as well as children. She gained favor with a number of interior designers who liked her paintings and commissioned her to do a series of Chinese-inspired scenes of birds and flowers on silk for their clients. As she became busier and happier, her hair color grew lighter. By the time we moved to South Dakota, when I was twelve, her hair was a Marilyn Monroe blonde.

All of the permutations in my mother's hair color seemed equally real to me when I was growing up. They were another facet of her personality, an extension of her mood. I once asked my grandmother, my mother's mother, if she could remember the natural color of my mother's hair—all the pictures of my mother's youth were in black and white and much faded. My grandmother closed her eyes in concentration, putting her forefinger into her soft, doughy cheek, before she finally decided that it had been a light honey color. But only from the age of twelve, she noted.

My mother had been born with thick, dark hair, in fact—as black as her father's, my grandmother said—but then at the age of eleven she contracted three life-threatening illnesses in a row: measles, scarlet fever, and rheumatic fever. She'd been bedridden and quarantined for months. Her dark, thick hair fell out, and when her hair grew back in, it had changed texture and color. She had become a blonde. My mother hated her hair then. The rest of her siblings had dark hair and brown eyes, and she felt like a freak. Now my mother had light hair to go with her green eyes. When my mother grew up, she decided to take matters into her own hands and change her hair color periodically. None of us thought it at all odd, not anyone in our family or hers, this chameleon relationship my mother had with her hair. She was an artist. Artists were supposed to do things like that, we figured. The same way professors moved their families from one end of the country to the other, in search of the next, new, more challenging position.

When we traveled to South Dakota for the first time in August 1979 to house hunt while my father signed his contract at the university, a real estate agent took us around the tiny town and my mother soon realized that the houses there were too small and too close, that living there would make a person claustrophobic. There was no point in moving from a tract house in New Jersey to a tract house in South Dakota, she decided, and she asked to be shown something in the country. That's how we found our farm.

It was a sight to behold—a tan brick house built into a hill, surrounded by four acres of Kentucky bluegrass, a sixteen-acre field for crops to the north, a stream that ran through a corner of the property, a thick grove in back, and seven trees around the hill, cottonwoods and box elders and a maple that turned Chinese red in autumn. The farm had belonged to a local property developer and he'd designed the house himself, including the landscaping, which was unusual for a farm, because trees sucked up water and took up space and didn't yield any profits. Most farmers weren't fond of trees unless they formed a windbreak from the winter storms, and our trees were merely stately and tall and picturesque. After he'd developed houses on all his other properties, he'd decided to move to greener pastures, and that's how this dream house happened to be on the market.

Because the house was built into the hill, both floors opened onto level ground, so that the house seemed like two ranch-style homes put together. On the lower level, my mother decided she could set up an art studio in the sunny yellow room that faced the stream and the giant cottonwoods on the neighbor's property, where horses were boarded.

My brother and I, suburban kids, had never imagined so much space to roam and play in. There were tree houses to be built, giant holes to be dug, go-cart tracks that could be constructed under the cool shade of the trees. We could hardly wait for our Siberian Husky from New Jersey to see this place. We imagined how strong we would grow as we explored our fields, testing our puny muscles in new and invigorating ways. Our friends in New Jersey wouldn't recognize us, we'd be so fit.

Although the days were very hot and dry in the summer, at night we would need no air conditioning, the real estate agent assured us. We could simply open the windows and let the wind blowing across the prairie sweep through our bedrooms.

Happily, my parents signed the papers. The farm was very inexpensive by New Jersey standards, where a quarter-acre could cost several hundred thousand dollars, but it was still a little pricey for my parents' salaries. They ended up having to use up all our liquid assets, including the small savings account I had opened a few years earlier as my "college fund." I was upset about losing my money, but my parents assured me that they'd be able to pay me back when the time came for me to actually attend college. What with my father's new position and the job that my mother had been offered at the university as well, we were all fairly confident that such an investment—in land, in a beautiful setting, in a solid house—would prove wise in the long run. Now, with a lovely farm waiting for us, we were all feeling more optimistic about the move.

Sure, there had been a few glitches when we'd visited the town of five thousand, which was smaller than any town we'd ever seen before in our lives. People had stared as we walked down the sidewalk, but my parents were able to laugh it off. We were newcomers, after all. And then there was the odd way the other vice presidents kept telling my father that this position was only a stepping-stone for him. Surely he'd want to leave in a couple years, perhaps move to the West Coast this time. After my father insisted that no, his wife and kids would love it here, all the good country air, the small-town lifestyle, that he was putting down roots this time, they had shaken their heads and laughed in what my father assumed was a good-natured way.

We moved in September, just after Labor Day. The first few weeks before all our boxes arrived, before we all grew extremely busy with work and school, before everything started to go wrong, were indeed blissful.

Our new house sat off a gravel road on a slight hill. We were only two miles from town limits, but we could not see the town from our fields. The property next door had a stream that ran through it onto our land, four or five tall cottonwoods, and a large white barn with red trim. The horses ran together in circles, their black manes and tails floating on the wind like wavy lines drawn in ink to accentuate their speed. Those horses were some of the most beautiful creatures I had ever seen. Sometimes they walked up to the barbed-wire fence that separated their grassy field from our brome field, and my brother and I would pick handfuls of brome and feed it to them. The horses ate daintily, pulling their lips back from their teeth as they plucked the grass from our fingers, and when they were finished they flicked their ears at us in thanks and went back to grazing in their field.

When our Husky arrived from New Jersey, the first thing he did was run from our yard into theirs. He was very fast in those days and we couldn't stop him. We called and called, frantically, afraid that Husky would be trampled to death or that he would frighten the horses and cause them injury in some way. But Husky ran right up to the horses and circled them, running faster and faster, until he was just a black-and-white blur, while the horses stood very still and watched. And after circling them for several minutes, he abruptly stopped.

A stallion stepped forward, tossing his mane and looking at our dog out of the corner of his large brown eyes. Husky took several steps toward the horse and then rose up on his hind legs and put his front paws on the horse's chest.

I hollered Husky's name as loudly as possible now because I was certain that such an action, a dog jumping upon a horse, would lead to violence. I didn't know anything about horses, of course. When had I ever even seen a real horse except on a field trip once, to a farm made up to resemble one from colonial American times—and those horses had been old and gentle and familiar with tourists and schoolkids and the indignities of being on display. Those horses sauntered up and ate apples and carrots from our hands and then trotted off, bored, farting and blowing snot from their nostrils, the minute they'd scarfed down our offerings. They had been fat and saggy and nothing like the horses in the field next door to us.

The only time I'd ever seen a dog jump on a horse before had been on a National Geographic special, and it had ended badly, with both animals being eaten. First the horse and then the dog. Actually, it hadn't been a horse and dog, exactly, but a zebra and a hyena, and there had been a pride of lions involved too, although they hadn't been in the camera shot to begin with but showed up at the very end, right before the commercial break. But as I stood there staring in fear at Husky and the stallion, I forgot these details, remembering only the grim, unhappy ending.

So I stood on our grassy hill, shouting hysterically, "Husky! Husky! Come back!"

Husky and the stallion ignored me completely. They both stood completely still, Husky with his paws on the horse's chest and the horse before him, both of them looking into each other's curious eyes.

And then, after what had to be a full minute, Husky dropped back onto all fours and turned around and ran back to us.

After that, he and the horses got along fine.

At night, I could hear the horses. They sounded as though they were in my bedroom. That close. I could hear them whinny and neigh and snort through their wet nostrils. I could hear them blow air over their teeth. I could hear their hooves picking through the hard soil where they had grazed all summer, and the softer sound as they plodded along the muddier ground near the stream. As the days grew chillier and the fallen leaves began to collect beneath the cottonwoods, I could hear them crunching through the ravine. Sometimes the wind would swell, making the trees shiver, and the horses would all run at once, round and round. As I lay in bed, listening to them run, my heart would beat faster, and as the wind swept through my room, brushing my hair from my forehead, causing the canopy on my bed to ripple, I could imagine I was running with the horses, the wind in our faces, the moonlight showing us a silver path to follow in the dark. Because I had never ridden a horse, I could not imagine what that would be like. I could only picture myself like our Husky, running with my feet on the ground.

Once I rose in the middle of the night, awakened by some instinct, and found my parents in the kitchen, seated on the barstools around the counter. My brother soon joined us. My mother fixed us cups of cocoa with marshmallows melted inside and we all sat in the living room on the carpet, as our furniture hadn't arrived yet, and watched the clouds race across the moon through the large picture window. In the dark night, everything rippled and flickered under the light of the moon, and it seemed to us that we were living on a small boat in a vast undulating sea. This was not a frightening image but rather one that tickled us. We felt very snug and secure on our boat.

My father put his arm around my mother's shoulders and she leaned her head back against his chest, and they seemed to sway together as they watched the world floating outside our window.

Autumn was a surprise, arriving just a few weeks after we did. The leaves on our cottonwoods turned a bright yellow overnight, as though ten thousand canaries had settled in the limbs sometime between sunset and dawn. We took to wearing our winter sweaters. Still, the sunlight was intense and warm, beguiling, seductive, and we couldn't imagine how cold it would become, or how quickly.

There were other surprises. For example, my mother's job. She was promised a position at the university when my father signed his contract. His salary was now actually less than what he had been earning at City College, despite the elevated rank, but my mother was told not to worry. She'd have a full-time position in public relations at the university to compensate. With two salaries, we could make it, no problem. Her job was to start in January, but after my mother went to campus that fall to fill out the paperwork, she was informed by one of the other vice presidents that there had been a misunderstanding. Her job was provisional on there being funds available, and there weren't any. She had a letter offering the job, a signed letter, and she shook it in the air before the vice president. He smiled like a cat and said he understood her disappointment. He sighed. He shook his head in apology, he pursed his lips. Maybe next year something will come up, he said.

My mother was furious, but nothing could ruin my father's helium mood. He was the vice president for academic affairs. He was the first Asian American to hold this position in the continental United States. His picture appeared on the front page of newspapers all over Taiwan. He gave interviews daily on the phone. He took to referring to himself in the third person around the house. "Vice President Chai is in his office if anyone calls." "Vice President Chai would like some tea." Or sometimes, just the litany "Vice President, Vice President Chai, Vice President, Vice President Chai," as though if he tried the title on enough, he'd break it in, like a pair of new shoes.

It was driving my mother nuts, this kind of talk, and once, in the middle of one of his sessions, she interrupted to announce that she was going to take a walk in the brome field. My brother and I watched her from the windows of the kitchen where we were still unpacking boxes, trying to find something to make dinner with. My mother marched up the green lawn to the edge of the golden field of swaying bromegrass and then headed down the path we'd trampled earlier. My little terrier, Betty, who rode all the way with us from New Jersey in our car, quickly ran to join her, as did the sleek, black-and-white cat that had wandered onto our property and refused to leave. Soon my mother was shrinking into the field, her blonde head bobbing determinedly in the distance.

My father quieted down now that my mother was out of the house. There was no use talking to himself, after all.

It didn't occur to him to run after her, to join her on her walk. My father liked the idea of owning a brome field, something vast to look at out the window and to call his own, but a field was not something he actually wanted to walk in.

When my mother returned in an hour or so, her skin flushed pink, wisps of brome and pollen and bits of yellow leaf in her hair, she was smiling.

We had all been anxious in her absence, my brother and I ripping through the kitchen boxes, my father pacing nervously. He couldn't function if my mother was upset. But now she was back and she was happy again and everything would be all right. We could all feel it. We could all breathe properly once more.

"Winberg, you have to come outside and feel the wind. You have to see the sunset!"

"No, no, no, I don't need to go outside." My father shook his head vigorously and flapped his arms as though to ward off flies. "I've been thinking, you don't need a job. You're going to be too busy. You're the wife of a vice president now. You're going to have to entertain and be a companion to the president's wife. We have to attend a lot of functions. You won't have time for another job."

I couldn't imagine how my father thought this would be comforting, and I winced from my position on the floor behind a pile of moving boxes, but my mother was too happy from her walk to argue.

"Come on, Mr. Vice President. Come and see the sunset."

"No, no." My father shook his head again but my mother had him by the arm now. She was pulling him to the door: "Doesn't Vice President Chai want to see the view from his new house? Come on, Mr. V.P. Let's go."

And then my father was laughing, and I heard the screen door creak open and then shut behind them.

When my brother and I ran to the living room to watch them through the front window, peering at them from behind the curtains, we found that they were walking hand in hand down the hill, the cat and my dog running after them. The sky was burning up with golds and reds, imperial colors, while the deep, jade-colored cornfield swayed in the wind, the sound like a vast ocean lapping at the edge of our property. We watched as our parents walked together to the end of our lawn, where the long gravel driveway met the gravel road, and then they stood together, my father's arm around my mother's shoulders, gazing at the sky.

Somehow the scene felt intensely private, as though we were watching our parents make love, or argue, something they wouldn't want my brother and me to see.

"Come on," I told my brother. "Let's finish unpacking."

And we both turned from the window and retreated to another stack of boxes.

8

Hunting Season

Often, that autumn, I woke up in the middle of the night with sharp pains radiating up and down my calves. I was twelve and growing rapidly. Soon hips would be jutting out where once I'd had straight lines, my waistline would shrink, breasts would bud, hair would appear in embarrassing places. My skin took on an unfamiliar sheen and developed a new smell. I didn't like what was happening to me. It was as though I'd followed Alice down the rabbit hole and eaten something I shouldn't have. I was growing in places, shrinking in others. I hardly knew what to make of myself.

In a matter of weeks, my feet wouldn't fit into my shoes. My good New Jersey shoes, I thought. The kind that matched exactly my best friend Theresa's shoes. We got them at the same time when Mrs. Gilfedder took us shopping for school clothes. I was leaving, moving away, but we were going to dress alike, just as though I were still there. And so Theresa bought two pairs of Lee jeans from the Jeans Depot in Pompton Plains, turquoise and pink, and I bought two as well, in pink and banana. She bought her shiny lamé bomber jacket in banana and I got mine in turquoise. She got striped black-and-white Adidas sneakers and blue suede dress shoes; ditto for me. This was what all the cool kids in junior high wore, and we were going to be cool, too. Not like in sixth grade, when we still wore clothes our mothers had ordered from the Sears catalog or, worse, sewn for us from scratch.

Now I woke up one morning and my good New Jersey shoes didn't fit. I hadn't even been gone a month. I wrote a letter to Theresa, dropping hints. I didn't want to say outright, I can't wear our shoes, what about you? But I asked her if she had any trouble keeping them clean and she replied, no, her father cleaned the suede for her on weekends. I knew then that there wasn't any chance she might be getting new shoes, shoes that we might be able to pick out together long distance. I was changing and my best friend was not.

The one shoe store in town was a disappointment. It was very small, and rather than specializing in children, let alone girls, it carried shoes for everybody, for every season, including work boots, cowboy boots, hunting boots, galoshes, slippers, sneakers, some of the plainest loafers I'd ever encountered in my life, and vinyl "dress" shoes. The shoe salesman lost the last shred of respect I had for him when he tried to sell me a pair of wedge heels with a hole cut out of the wedge. Didn't he know that those were just so fifth grade?

"All the other girls in junior high are wearing them," he promised me, but I was having none of it.

I couldn't believe that our town was two years behind the fashion cycle, at least.

My mother tried to make excuses for me, and I went over to examine the three styles of sneakers. That's when the salesman made his second big mistake.

"Hey, aren't you living in the O'Brien place?" he asked my mother.

"No," she replied. "It's our place now."

"Well, just the same. Nice place. I was thinking of driving out there this weekend and shooting me a pheasant."

"Oh, I'm sorry. We don't allow hunting on our property."

"Why, sure you do! It's the law. I can hunt anywhere I want."

"No, I'm afraid you're wrong. The law states that there's no hunting on private property that's been posted. And there's no hunting within three hundred feet of a house. We've already marked our fields, and the area around our house is off limits as well."

There had been several articles about the start of the hunting season in the local paper and my mother had read them carefully. She herself did not approve of guns or shooting. She had wanted to make sure our property would be safe for our dogs and for my brother and me. There was no point in moving to the country if we couldn't be free to roam on our own property. We'd bought a dozen "No Hunting" signs from the Ben Franklin's and spent the weekend posting them around our fields. My mother was quite sure of her rights.

But the shoe salesman was undeterred. "That's not the law. You have no idea what you're talking about, lady." And he started to laugh.

I could see out of the corner of my eye that my mother did not like the way he had said "lady." She drew herself up to her full height, fists on her hips, pointy elbows sticking out like the quills of a porcupine. "Young man," my mother began, her voice calm but firm, "I will call the sheriff immediately if anyone should come near my property with a gun! And I *will* prosecute!"

Then she turned on her heel. "Come on. We're leaving."

I had to run to keep up with her as she threw open the door in a fury and stalked out to our car.

Later, we'd get my shoes in Sioux City, Iowa, where there was a mall with many shoe stores, people who didn't stare, and certainly no one who threatened to shoot on our property. I had to endure my pinched toes for another couple weeks until we had time to make the forty-mile trip to Iowa, but I didn't mind at all.

The next day a cold wind blew through town and the leaves seemed to fall from the trees all at once. When we'd gone to bed, they were still dangling from the cottonwoods, but the next morning the lawn and driveway were carpeted with their shriveled brown bodies. This created a new problem for my mother. We had acres and acres of lawn and no time to rake it. We still had boxes to unpack and the house to organize, my father was at work all the time, and my brother and I had a lot of make-up homework, as we'd started the school year late on account of the move. My mother found that she had little time for extra chores, for she was indeed expected to be a companion to the president's wife, volunteering in all the same groups. And, for my father's sake, she had to entertain more and more, cooking enormous elaborate banquets, using recipes from the

New York Times Magazine, which we still subscribed to. My parents couldn't break the *Times* habit, even though the papers arrived not daily but once a week through the mail, five or six at a time, sometimes soggy and illegible. The *Times* recipes were extremely complicated, European affairs with lists of ingredients seventeen, nineteen items long. They took hours to prepare. There was no such thing as timesavers in those days. Even TV dinners took fifty-five minutes to bake in the oven. Not that a hostess would ever consider cutting corners. Executives' wives who read the Sunday *Times Magazine* were supposed to entertain in style.

We'd always raked our own leaves in New Jersey, but it was impossible now, and my mother didn't want the lawn to die, all that beautiful bluegrass, so she called Job Services and they sent two young men to rake the lawn.

They were young Lakota men "from West river," they said, which we'd learned by now meant the part of the state west of the Missouri. They were polite and neatly dressed, with long black braids and plaid work shirts tucked into their jeans. My brother and I spotted them the moment the school bus dropped us off at the end of our driveway. Our dog, Husky, and the adopted cat were poised near the men, watching intently as they bagged the leaves that had collected in the ditches, a river of leaves. More leaves than we had ever seen at one place. We waved to the men as we ran up the driveway and they waved back. We called to our pets and our pets glanced our way but didn't move. They preferred to stay with the Indians.

All afternoon my brother couldn't stop talking about the Indians. There was nothing cooler than Indians in New Jersey. In our school in Pequannock there had been one Iroquois family who stayed for a couple years, and they were like celebrities. You would have thought they'd just stepped off the set of a John Wayne movie, the way the rest of us acted around them. When had we ever seen Indians except on TV?

For my brother, having Indians at our house was like having movie stars show up. He couldn't believe it.

That evening after dinner, my father allowed my brother to call his best friend, Victor, back in New Jersey just so that he could tell him, even though it was a school night, not to mention a long-distance call (and we were only allowed to make long-distance calls on weekends, and then only once a month—our parents had been very clear about this).

The next day, however, our house drew a crowd.

As soon as the Indians showed up for work, cars and pickups began to cruise in front of our property. They didn't barrel down the road like the three cars that passed on our road with any frequency—the mailman, the bus driver, and our next-door neighbors. No, these vehicles slunk by. They slowed to a crawl, as though in the worst rush-hour traffic. The drivers craned their necks.

The Indians worked quickly and finished the job that afternoon. My mother was surprised; she had thought it would take four days, at least, and the young men had concurred. But now they asked for their pay and left quickly, without lingering to accept the tea and sandwiches that my mother had prepared for them.

It wasn't long before my mother started receiving the phone calls. The first was from a woman down the road from us, roughly a mile away; she lived on top of a hill on the oil-top road. (No one said "asphalt" in our town.) She said she was only calling out of common decency to warn my mother. Didn't my mother know what happened to the last woman who'd been foolish enough to hire an Indian to work for her? She'd been found with her throat slit.

"The Indians are just waiting for their chance to break into your home and bleed you to death. They've done it before. Last year or the year before. To a jeweler and his wife," the woman continued breathlessly. I listened with my head pressed against my mother's, the receiver between us.

"Oh, but surely that can't be true," my mother said, laughing.

"You don't know," the woman said. "You're not from around here. When an Indian is drunk, you can't tell. He remains completely still, his face just like a mask, and then suddenly he goes berserk and tries to kill you."

"Well! That would be something!"

"You don't know," the woman said again. Then she hung up.

More phone calls. A woman who volunteered with Welcome Wagon in town, another who claimed to have met my mother at one of the university gatherings, anonymous people.

"We have to stick together," said the final person to call before my mother decided to stop answering the phone. "You have to know which side you're on."

"It's like a comedy—I feel like I'm in a movie!" my mother exclaimed, turning to me as she set the phone back on its hook.

"Do you think it's true?" I asked anxiously. It seemed preposterous, what all those callers had said, but then again I knew nothing about this part of the country. "What if they're right?"

My mother sighed, but she didn't look particularly worried. Tired, mostly. "Well, I guess we'll find out, won't we? Don't worry. We're in God's hands."

And then the phone rang again. But this time it was my father. We heard his voice calling from the answering machine, "Hello? Hello? Are you home?" He had some kind of dinner party to attend and he was calling my mother to ask if she could meet him there. He was working late and wouldn't have time to come home first.

After my mother had changed her clothes and fixed her hair, she left my brother and me, kissing us on the foreheads before she ran out the door, the scent of her perfume lingering in the air.

My brother sat forlornly at the kitchen counter while I put two TV dinners in the oven. "Some people called and said the Indians were going to come back and try to kill us," I said.

"Cool!"

"No, for real they are."

My brother got up from his stool and ran to the living room in the front of the house so that he could look out onto the neatly raked front lawn through our large picture window. He squatted on his heels. "When are they coming?"

"Probably this evening. When it's dark."

He nodded. "That's when I'd do it, too."

"We won't be able to hear them. They're very quiet. They can break inside without making a sound. We won't even know they're here until it's too late. And then it's—chhhht!" I drew a finger across my throat.

"Are they going to shoot us with arrows or scalp us with tomahawks?"

I thought about this for minute. "Neither. They use knives nowadays."

"Hmm." My brother looked thoughtful. He rested his chin upon his fist and leaned his forehead against the window. "I wish they'd hurry up and come back."

"You're sick."

"They wouldn't do anything to me. I'm going to join them," he announced.

It was no use. I couldn't frighten my little brother. I left him in the living room and went back into the kitchen. I turned on the small black-and-white TV we kept on the counter and watched a rerun of *M*A*S*H*. Hawkeye and B.J. were conspiring to play a trick on that insufferable prig, Frank Burns. They needed to borrow a dress from Klinger, who made them pay with supplies stolen with the aid of feckless Radar, when uptight Margaret caught them all in the act. She was threatening to report them and have them all court-martialed when the sound of choppers interrupted everything and they all ran to the hospital tents to prepare for the incoming wounded. Every episode of *M*A*S*H* was like this, which was why I liked the show so much. The repetition and predictability added a sense of stability to my life that was otherwise completely absent.

After the show ended, my brother got tired of waiting for the Indians and came back into the kitchen to eat his TV dinner. After dinner we unpacked a few boxes of our father's books in the basement. Then we played a game of ping-pong. Still, our parents hadn't returned.

We went back upstairs and crouched on the carpet by the picture window, lying low so that hopefully nobody out there would see us. Now that it was dark, my brother was a little more nervous, though not really scared. The night was darker here in the countryside than in New Jersey. There were no streetlights or neighbors' houses with windows lit up from within. Our back field had some light from the mercury-vapor lamp that stood just north of our house, but the picture window faced east, into the vast dark expanse of our lawn and the even darker remnants of the harvested corn field that lay just across the road and extended all the way to the horizon. After we had stared into the dark long enough, we could just make out the different shades of our charcoal lawn and the obsidian trees, the ashy color of the split-rail fence and the grayish bromegrass waving in the inky ditch. The sky darkened and the moon rose and the stars shone like diamonds.

When our parents finally returned from their party, they found us sitting by the window, waiting for the Indians to come back and kill us. Of course, we didn't tell them that that's what we were doing.

My mother assumed we were lonely. "Did you miss us?" she cried out, hugging us to her. I noticed that she no longer smelled like perfume but rather of cigarette smoke, sweat, and other people's greasy food.

We all went to bed shortly after they returned, but in the middle of the night, when I crept out of my bed and whispered in my doorway to my brother's room across the hall, "Are you awake?" he replied immediately, "Are you?"

"I don't think the Indians are coming," I whispered.

"Probably not tonight." He sighed.

"Better go to sleep," I said.

"You too."

I crept back into my bed, pleased to know that I wasn't the only one who couldn't sleep, slipped beneath my covers, and dozed off almost at once.

My brother and I waited for the Indians to return every day that week, but in the end it wasn't the Indians who came shooting at our house.

The first time it happened, it was the middle of the night. I had been drowsing, not quite awake, not yet fully asleep, although my daydreams had begun to take a new form, seeping out of my head and spilling into my darkened room. My bed had begun to wobble around the edges and then gradually dissolved, until I was sitting on the avocado-colored sofa in our family room in New Jersey, reading by the standing lamp, while my brother lay on the floor playing with his toy soldiers. He'd lined the army-green plastic men up and down the floor in columns and along the arms of the sofa and the top of the cabinet where my mother kept her fabrics for sewing projects. He seemed to have an endless supply, because just as he finished one column, he began another, until soldiers limned the baseboard heaters and the top of the television set, and finally he set them on the tops of my blue suede shoes. I wanted to shake them off, they irritated me like ants, but he pleaded, "Don't move, don't move!" as he set the soldiers one after another in a line up my legs to my knees. Then the wind picked up in the trees outside my window, and in my semiconscious state I could hear their leaves rustling like taffeta. I turned over in my bed without thinking, moving into the cool breeze, and suddenly my heart jerked and I thought, "Oh, no! I've knocked all the soldiers over!" And sure enough, the soldiers were tumbling in lines, like dominoes, falling all around me, as my brother whimpered and scurried across the floor, trying to set them upright, trying to stop the lines from tumbling into each other, but his hand was always a second too slow and the soldiers continued to fall. They seemed larger than I remembered and I tried to brush them off my skin as they fell and fell, faster and thicker, like the box elder bugs that clung to the glass of the front windows of our house, the windows that faced the cornfield, squirming and trembling in the hot sun. We were shocked to come home from school one day and find the house covered in the black-and-red bugs. They were dying in their trees at the base of our driveway, the air was growing too cool for them, but the sun against the glass was warm, and they clung to the windows as if for life. But they all died anyway, in a few weeks, their bodies littering our sidewalk. My mother swept them up with a broom.

The wind grew louder, a sudden insistent hum.

The soldiers are going to be crushed, I thought sleepily. We must clear them out of the street, for suddenly it seemed that my brother was playing in the middle of our dirt road, lining his soldiers up in the ruts and ridges that formed there from the heavy tractors and the bus and the pickups that passed. I sat up in bed with my eyes still closed with the vague feeling that I must warn my brother to move, a car was coming.

The sound was unmistakable: a car was indeed barreling down our road, and I came fully awake just as the shot rang out.

At first, when I gasped, I thought my heart had stopped. I felt a pain in my chest as though my heart had been ripped from my body. I clutched at it then, pushing at my ribs through my nightgown, pressing on my skin with all ten fingers, as though I might be able to feel my heart, as though I might be able to replace it with my hands, if only I could find where it had fallen.

My brother was crying.

My parents were running through the hallway; suddenly their footsteps sounded very loud. I hadn't realized they could clomp about so; I'd always thought of my parents as light-footed. Now they were at my door, both of them at once, rushing in together, squeezing through the tiny doorway. My door hit the wall with a smack.

"Are you okay? Is everything all right?" they shouted and without waiting for an answer they rushed across the hall into my brother's room.

The lights flashed on in the hall. My mother ran to the kitchen, my father's hand jerked through the doorway and turned on my light. I blinked.

He and my brother stared at me with white faces.

Obediently, I got up from my bed and followed them to the kitchen, where we sat and waited while my mother talked on the phone with the sheriff's office.

I don't remember now whether the sheriff or a deputy came out that evening or whether they convinced my mother that there was nothing that could be done now, the shooters were gone, we couldn't describe the car, there was no reason to come in the middle of the night. Maybe they came the next day, or maybe they didn't come at all. Maybe it was only my father who walked around our house and up and down our hill, trying to see where the bullet had struck.

Now, after all these years, I remember only how I felt that night, as we sat huddled together, our skin looking strange and sallow under the kitchen lights, as I watched my mother's narrow back while she stood arguing into the phone, the thin cotton of her yellow nightgown stretched tight over her shoulders, and my heart at last began to beat again.

When the men came to shoot during the day, it was usually on the pretext of hunting, although it was unclear to me what they thought they were going to catch. It was pheasant season, but there were no pheasants on our property, none in the freshly mown ditches before our driveway, certainly none lurking on our bluegrass-covered hill, none in the empty cornfields that had long since been harvested. It was legal to hunt deer and elk and moose and caribou with the right kind of licenses, but there were none of those animals in our fields. The farmers' combines would have scared them away. It was also possible to hunt mourning doves, but the birds disappeared soon after the start of the hunting season, as though by some internal clock, and only black crows, some as large as cats, could be seen circling over the empty fields, hoping to find some forgotten ears of corn.

The law had been revised the year we arrived, and it was no longer legal to shoot within three hundred feet of a house. There had indeed been an article in the local paper about this, and my mother reminded the sheriff about the new law every time she called him to complain about the men shooting near our house. But we soon discovered that every law contained two parts, the part that was written down and the part that could be enforced. The shoe salesman had understood this completely. It was my mother who hadn't understood at all.

My mother spoke with other farm families, and they all decried these weekend hunters. *Real* hunters took gear and tents to the Black Hills to hunt the big game, or what was left of it. These local men merely got drunk, drove around, and shot at things. One farmer complained that he'd had to spend $10,000 to repair an irrigation system in one of his fields. It had been shot full of holes. He recommended that my mother buy some guns herself. "If they come up on your property, you can shoot back," he said. That was the only way he was able to protect his cattle sometimes.

My mother thanked him for his advice, but she wouldn't buy any guns.

My brother and I took to watching these fake hunters when they drove by. We crouched low on the floor and peered from behind the edges of the curtains of our front window. As we were uncertain what they were hunting for, we didn't want to provide a target.

The men appeared quite drunk and uncertain themselves as to what they were shooting at. They seemed to be shooting just to be shooting. Just to intimidate. Just to make loud noises. And to make them outside our house.

Sometimes they shouted out their windows as they shot. Words like "Jap!" Words like "Cunt!" Sometimes they just made strange, animal-like noises that stretched in the wind and turned into a howl.

When the men came by shooting, our mother made my brother and me stay indoors.

Although they rarely shot at night, not after that first terrifying time, I found that I now had trouble sleeping, a problem that would haunt me for decades, well after I had left South Dakota, gone on to college, traveled the world. At night I would return to my twelve-year-old self, my ears buzzing.

My bedroom was at the front of the house and I could hear a car coming from a great distance, its tires crunching atop the gravel, first very far away and then, as the sound grew louder, I could tell the car or pickup was approaching, faster and faster. And then I held my breath. Would the car speed by with a whoosh that sent a cloud of dust and pebbles into the air, traveling over the wind and breaking against the glass of my window in a crackle? Or would it begin to slow, the crunching sound of its tires growing louder, like teeth gnashing bones, like glass breaking beneath a heavy weight? And then, if it slowed, would men shout from their windows at our house? Would they howl like a sick coyote? Would they shoot?

9

The Little Things

At first, it was the little things that began to drive my father crazy. Not the big ones, not the staring or the shooting, if you can imagine, but the mundane, everyday details. For example, the food. He'd forgotten this aspect about life away from New York, how people could live without Chinese food. Later he'd kick himself, but by then it was too late.

Our first few months in South Dakota we used to drive hours just to try a new Chinese restaurant. Sixty-five miles to Sioux Falls, 130 miles round-trip, just because he saw an ad in the yellow pages for Peking duck. Well, it was a duck all right, but not from Peking. Eighty miles round-trip to Iowa on a rumor of Szechwan-style chicken. Instead we'd find a tiny diner, run by a single family, the menu offering dishes we'd heard about in jokes but never imagined could actually exist. Egg foo young. Beef chop suey. Stir-fried rice made with mixed vegetables and Spam. The proprietors were always polite, overly so; they treated us like long-lost family, my father like a brother who'd been missing for years and then suddenly turned up on their doorstep—they were so surprised to see another Chinese face. They fawned over my brother and me. They gave us free egg rolls, extra spareribs, dessert on the house. And though we smiled and promised to return, praising their awful food, I could tell my father was lying as he forced their food down his throat without chewing.

Once, during a faculty meeting shortly after my father had taken his post at the university, he was introduced to the resident China Hand. A short man of considerable girth, he'd never actually been to China, nor could he read or speak Chinese. But he'd been to Taiwan once on a grant from the Nationalist government, which had made him expert enough to self-publish an academic book on his travels. He liked "Oriental things" and had many good forgeries of famous paintings on the walls of his office. He also apparently liked Chinese women, and after a drink or two, or three, he would regale listeners with his tales of carousing with Asian prostitutes from his navy days.

He wasn't too pleased to meet my father, I could tell. He was no longer the expert. Still, he sidled up to my dad at a party at our house once, drink in hand, leaning close to his cheek, one thick hand on my father's shoulder. "Tell me, Winberg, why is it," the China Hand asked, his words slightly slurred, his breath spraying wetly against my father's neck, "why it is that the Chinese could create five thousand years of continuous civilization and yet have such lousy food? You'd think they'd have learned how to fix a steak by now!"

Later, after everyone else had gone home, we laughed together as a family, as though the man had been telling a joke, but even though my father opened his mouth and made a laughing sound, I could tell that he didn't actually think it was funny.

In New York he'd taken the food for granted. After six years of dining out with my grandparents, my uncles, our families, every weekend, he thought he'd never miss it. He was tired of the city, he'd told us. Worn out. All that MSG. The noise of Chinese restaurants. The smells. The crowds, the lines, the price for parking. Nothing was worth this, he said. But thirteen hundred miles away from Chinatown's mitten crabs and sizzling prawns, Shanghai-style "little dragon" soup dumplings, pork *baozi,* lion's head meatballs, braised greens, winter melon soup, smelly bean curd, red-cooked *doufu, ma po doufu, gong bao ji ding,* Buddha's delight, eight treasure rice, Hainan chicken, steamed ginger-sauce fish, his body began to go into withdrawal.

At first it was little things, barely noticeable. The way his mouth would suddenly go dry in the middle of the day. No matter how many glasses of water he drank, he felt parched. And then his right hand began to tremble, just the thumb and first two fingers, his chopsticks fingers. I'd watch them shake at dinner, as we ate our steaks and fries. Later he admitted to my mother that he was beginning to have daydreams that interrupted his thoughts. Right in the middle of a meeting, the president would be speaking, or another of the vice presidents, and suddenly the image of a piping hot bowl of longevity noodles, with shrimp floating on the glistening broth, maybe a few tender leaves of bok choy, would invade his mind, the fragrance of spring chicken and ginger wafting unmistakably into his nostrils. He clenched his fists then, he said, he pushed the point of a pencil against his own flesh, he stomped on one foot with the heel of the other, anything to try to dispel the image and focus his mind again. But nothing worked. When you begin to hallucinate about Chinese food, you know you're in trouble.

And so he began writing letters to his friends, dropping hints. He couldn't just out and out ask my grandparents for food, because he didn't want them to worry. And he couldn't call my uncles, because he was sure they would make fun of him. My mother tried to make some dishes but she'd never learned to cook Chinese food—there'd never been the need—and besides, the ingredients were unavailable in our town. So he wrote to colleagues, reminiscing about the meals they had shared together. Some of them recognized his desperation and sent food. Boxes of mooncakes. Tins of tea. Packages of rice noodles. Two former grad students from Taiwan sent him a gallon tub of *rou sung*. That's when I knew that he had really fallen off the deep end.

"You're eating too fast! You're going to choke!" I stood beside him in the kitchen, in case I should need to perform the Heimlich maneuver, which I'd just learned in school.

"Winberg, try to chew your food." My mother stood beside me, wringing her hands. "My goodness, your cheeks look like a chipmunk's."

Rou sung is a simple snack, nothing fancy; you can buy it in any Chinese grocery. It's desiccated pork that's been fried in lard, salt, and MSG. You're supposed to use it as a flavoring for *xi-fan*, for example, that is, soupy rice congee. You dip a little of the fried, shredded pork into your rice and (according to my father) it tastes delicious, the yin-yang blend of blandness and saltiness, the perfect combination of crunchy, stringy pork and smooth rice soup. But he took to eating the *rou sung* without the rice, which was neither natural nor healthy. The problem with making *xi-fan,* we discovered, was the hard rice available in the local grocery store. The Piggly Wiggly had only Minute Rice, Rice-a-Roni, Uncle Ben's, and small packages of dry American long grain, which never softened. You could leave it in water for days and then boil it for over an hour, adding water all the time, and still not get a decent bowl of congee. At worst, a strange gray scum would form on the surface of the water and the whole thing would have to be thrown away; at best the rice became somewhat less rocklike but the grains remained stubbornly separatist.

So my father took to eating the *rou sung* by itself, tablespoon after tablespoon, and soon developed canker sores all along his tongue and the lining of his cheeks. He began to lisp when he spoke, his mouth was so inflamed, but still he couldn't stop himself from eating more. He even took to hiding the containers at the very back of the refrigerator to keep us from eating any.

"You're being a pig!" I announced. "You're making yourself sick! That stuff is disgusting!" I tried to shame him into giving up his *rou sung,* but he ate the entire gallon in a matter of weeks.

Then more things began to bother my father. The pace of life, for example. He had hoped to make a lot of changes quickly, he had pressed the president to do so. He said he wanted to "globalize the curriculum," create core requirements, including a foreign language requirement; he wanted to expand study abroad programs. He gave a lot of interviews to the local papers explaining why these were positive things, how the "good people of South Dakota" needed to get out and see the world. He meant well, but he came off as arrogant.

The state was slow to fund the improvements he wanted. The regents didn't see the need, and the governor was playing hardball.

He'd already threatened to close one college and turn it into a prison (which in fact he did, a few years later).

My father invited colleagues from the East Coast to come for a new presidential lecture series he'd devised, in which the university would bring cosmopolitan speakers to campus, expose everyone to new points of view. The first semester was an eclectic season featuring Hawaii's East West Center president Victor Li, distinguished Yale historian Robin Winks, the *Time* magazine publishing magnate Henry Luce III, a noted scholar of African American literature and his former dean at City College, Theodore Gross, and the renowned Chinese American author Anna Chennault. She'd just published a memoir of her life in China during World War II and her husband's involvement with the Flying Tigers. I remember her visit to campus very well. She gave an exciting speech, full of anecdotes about General Stillwell and Generalissimo Chiang Kai-shek, their legendary feuds, as well as her own narrow escapes from Japanese bombing raids. After her talk she took questions from the audience. The China Hand asked if all the stories he'd heard about her husband's whoring were true. Mrs. Chennault was a practiced public speaker and handled the situation deftly, replying with a dismissive laugh that some people had active imaginations, but I felt my cheeks turn hot and quickly pressed my hands against them so that no one could see them turn a flaming red. My whole body broke into a sweat, I felt so embarrassed. At another event, a famous English professor whom my father had invited to campus was asked publicly if he was ready to accept the Lord Jesus Christ as his personal savior. The professor was Jewish and didn't appreciate the question.

Although it wasn't his fault, I know my father felt responsible. Even I felt responsible. We were the hosts; these were our guests. All of the speakers had stayed in our house. From my seat in the audience, I wanted to sink into the floor.

My father stopped referring to himself in the third person as "the Vice President." He stopped laughing and making jokes, too. He wore a worried look on his face that was entirely new.

If we drove to town and were stuck behind one of the slow-moving farm vehicles that crept along at fifteen miles per hour, my father would swear and shake. Sometimes he'd honk his horn, over and over, although of course the tractor wasn't going to speed up. Now, when people stopped on the sidewalks to turn and stare, I understood why.

Little things began to drive him nuts. The slow way merchants in town rang up purchases, stopping to chat with every customer; the way men smiled at my mother and called her "Blondie," flirting with her even in my father's presence; the fact that the town barber couldn't figure out how to cut my father's straight, wiry hair and ended up sculpting it into a strange, prickly helmet; the waves of dust that blew across our house every time a pickup truck sped down our gravel road. And then there were the snow storms that began in November and didn't let up until March or April, dumping a foot or two at a time, the snow forming high drifts that never melted. "I feel like I'm living on the moon!" my father complained.

The state didn't use de-icing chemicals to clear the roads because they caused the undersides of vehicles to rust, so the roads were always icy and packed with snow. My mother's Buick Skylark slid sideways across the state highway that circled our town, scaring all of us, so my father insisted she get a new car. He bought her a Jeep with four-wheel drive, although I knew my parents hadn't wanted to take on the cost of a new vehicle so soon after our move. We'd had so many expenses. My father began to worry about money. My mother still wanted to get a job, but in a town this small there weren't any opportunities for her, only openings for waitresses and salesclerks. The only big business was the university.

At dinner, my father began to complain to no one in particular, talking as though to the air. "I shouldn't have come here. I didn't want to leave the city, but I left for my family's sake." He sighed dramatically. "Yep, I did it for them. If I had my way, I'd live in a penthouse. I didn't want to live on a farm!"

Sometimes I'd grow angry and remind him that I hadn't wanted to move. I had wanted to stay in New Jersey with my friends.

Then my father said I was brat.

I ran to my room.

Later he would apologize. He would stand outside my bedroom door and say that he was sorry. I wouldn't reply. I'd sit with my arms wrapped about my knees, silent, holding my breath and listening, my ear to the door, until I heard his footsteps go back down the hall. Only then would I allow myself to cry.

10 The Closet

When I arrived home from school each day on the bus, I was in no mood to talk to my parents. My mother would ask, "How was school today? What did you do today? What did you learn?" And I'd reply angrily, "Leave me alone!" or "Nothing!" or "What are you always asking me that for?"

When my father got home from work, he asked the same questions. I couldn't stand it. Sometimes I would grow angry first, sometimes he would, but in the end it didn't matter how they began, because our fights always ended the same way. He shouted that I was not respectful, and I ran to my room and slammed the door.

Once my father came running down the hallway after me. He tried to open my door and I watched the knob turning. I could hear the metal click open and shut, open and shut. I could feel the wood vibrate against my back. There was no lock, but I sat on the floor, my back to the door, my feet braced against my bed. He pushed but the door would not open.

"Open the door!"

"No! Go away!"

I could hear my father breathing through the thin wood barrier. I imagined his sweaty, red face, his black eyebrows scrunching together in the middle of his forehead, his lips pressed into a thin, tight line. He stood there waiting for a long time. Then he tried the knob again, but I wouldn't budge and the door wouldn't open.

I could hear my mother's voice from the kitchen, calling to my father. He shuffled down the hall, his backless slippers slap-slap-slapping against the carpet. I rested my head against my knees and waited.

He came back. "I'm sorry," he said. He paused. I could hear the last intake of breath and then silence. He was holding his breath.

I almost forgave him, and then he tried my doorknob again. This time he was frustrated, his anger returning. He shook the knob, pounded on the door. "Open up, open up! What's the matter with you? Honor your father and mother! Honor your father and mother!" he shouted.

"Go away, go away! Go-away-go-away-go-away!" I kept shouting, over and over, as loudly as possible, until my throat felt raw, as though my skin were splintering, slivers of flesh tearing loose and dropping down the back of my throat. My temples throbbed. I narrowed my eyes into slits and balled my hands into fists, my body taut, my legs rigid at the knee as I pressed my back against the door.

Finally I realized that my father had gone away and I stopped shouting. My door was no longer vibrating against my back, bumping my spine. I held my breath for a minute to be sure, listening, in case it was a trick, but I heard nothing. Slowly I moved away from the door and lay flat on my stomach so that I could peer under the door. The carpet was so high, I couldn't really see anything. I put my ear to the crack, and then I heard my brother whisper, "Let me in."

I jumped as though it were a snake rattling. I dropped onto my stomach, patting down the carpet with my fingers. Sure enough, I could see a shadow there, and when I turned my head onto my right ear and looked out of the very corner of my eye, so that my eyeballs began to hurt, I could just make out the pink fleshy contours of his lips. He was on his belly in the hallway, trying to peer under my door.

I kicked the door sharply with my foot. I hoped it hit him. My brother got up and tried the knob, but I was too fast for him. I was back on the floor, legs braced against the bed.

He gave up easily, though, and disappeared into his room, which was directly opposite mine, our doors facing each other, only three feet apart.

I was glad he was gone, I told myself, and wrapped my arms around my knees and sat with my back against the door, feeling sorry for myself.

I cried a little, experimenting to see if this would make me feel better. At first it did, because my feelings of martyrdom were intensified. I pretended that I was deathly ill and imagined my parents crying at my funeral. Everyone was there, all my friends from New Jersey, our neighbors, my cousins. I could see my grandparents looking at my father with disgust, with anger. *How could he have treated May-lee so badly when she was alive?* They glared at him. My father hung his head. He could think of nothing to say to defend himself. I cried some more, thinking how sad it was that I was dead at age twelve. My mother was disconsolate, weeping before a large photograph of me by the coffin, covered with flowers, not ugly lilies or carnations, but my favorites, pansies and irises and lavender lilacs. My brother blubbered like a baby again, his cheeks trembling with grief.

I made myself cry harder, feeling terribly sorry for my short, wasted life, but then, in the next minute, I regretted all the crying. My sinuses started to throb. I was never able to cry very well because I had inherited my father's inefficient sinuses. At age forty-five he had to take sinus medication daily just to get them to drain; otherwise the pressure built up and made him feel as though paper were stuffed up his nose. He got headaches, watery eyes. He said it was because his mother used to put a clothespin on the bridge of his nose when he was a child, hoping she could make it grow taller. "My mother ruined my sinuses," he used to tell anyone who would listen, his doctors, his brothers, us. But when I cried, I realized that my sinuses were useless too. They exhibited all of his symptoms, and then there was a throbbing pain behind my eyeballs. This had nothing to do with my grandmother, I realized, it was just bad genes. My father's genes.

I stopped crying, but I felt angry at my father all over again.

Then I heard a strange, muffled sound coming from my closet. I imagined it was a mouse and my heart froze in my chest. For a full minute, I completely forgot about the pain in my sinuses as I listened to the strange, scratching sound. So regular, so persistent. And growing louder.

I leapt up off the floor and flung my door open. I ran across the hall into my brother's room. "Jeff, there's a mouse in my closet!" I shouted, but my brother was gone. His room was as small as mine, with less furniture, so there were not many places to hide. I had a canopy bed, a white-and-gold dresser from Sears, a pink comfy rocking chair, a more serious straight-backed chair, and a roll-top wooden desk. I had wanted a roll-top desk ever since third grade, when I read *Little Women* and discovered that Jo had one. I was going to be a writer, too, and so I had decided I needed a roll-top as well. Finally, in sixth grade, I'd gotten my wish.

My brother, however, had only his bunk beds and the same tiny dresser he'd had since he was a baby. He wasn't interested in furniture.

He wasn't under his bed and he couldn't fit into his dresser. I was ready to run out again when my brother emerged from his closet, holding his tiny penknife.

"Look," he said proudly, "I made a hole."

His round face was flushed. At eleven, he still had his baby fat, and a bowl cut, which only made his face look rounder. My mother kept promising she'd change the style, but she trimmed his bangs regularly. Even at the barber shop, this was all they could manage.

Now he sucked in his tiny red lips until his mouth was no larger than a fish's. "Look," he pleaded.

"Move," I barked. As the older sister, I didn't have to be polite. My brother obediently rolled out of the way and I squatted inside his closet. He didn't have many clothes, either, so his closet was a lot roomier than mine. I slid across the wood floor, wondering what I was supposed to be looking at.

"What?" I asked at last.

Eagerly he squeezed into the closet beside me. Then he pointed to a small dark square in the white pasteboard wall. It was a hole, I realized. And it led directly into my closet. Since our rooms were at the end of the hallway, they shared a common wall, which had now been breached. When I put my hand through, I could feel the pleats of my winter skirt.

"Hey!" I said, and my brother broke into giggles. When he laughed, he looked like the Buddha, everything jiggling, the rolls of flesh at his belly shaking along with his cheeks.

At eleven, my brother could not bear to be apart from me. He wanted to be near me all the time. He didn't want me to lock him out of my room. Now he had drilled a hole in our closets. I decided that he was nuts, and I was about to tell him off when suddenly I realized that my brother knew. He understood my mood because he was going through the same thing at school. Only it was worse, because boys had to prove themselves by punching, whereas with girls, it's only words. "Only" words. Hadn't we all learned the difference: sticks and stones may break my bones, but words will never hurt me? Still, they meant the same thing, the words the girls said at school and the punches the boys delivered.

I decided not to tell my brother off, and I didn't tell our parents about the hole he made, either.

Over the next few days, Jeff enlarged the hole in the closet until it was a veritable window. Now, when my father got angry, when we retreated to our rooms, we could sit in our closets and talk. When my mother came to look for us, we held our breaths, hiding in silence until she gave up trying to find us and went away. They didn't understand us, but we didn't need them. We had each other.

At twelve, I thought this connection would last forever. My brother would always be little, a child, he would be my smiling Buddha forever.

But soon, sooner than I expected, he would take an interest in clothes and they would fill his closet, and his friends' company would replace mine, and he would stuff up the hole between our closets, and we'd both forget it was even there.

Then we would both really be alone.

Things I learned from kids in school:

"Jew" was a verb.

People with darker skin looked like that because they were dirty.

Dark-skinned dirty people were more likely to be criminals than anyone else.

There was no such thing as green eyes. There were only blue eyes, brown eyes, and dirty blue eyes. (My mother and brother had dirty blue eyes.)

I must have been adopted, because I didn't look like my mother.

Mixed-race people are signs of the End Times, when the Anti-Christ would return and rule on earth for a thousand years of bloodshed and turmoil. The presence of my brother and me in school and in town was definitely Not a Good Sign.

My mother was a floozy, because what kind of white woman would marry a Chinaman, anyway?

Chinaman was an acceptable term.

Floozy was an acceptable term.

Gut and *Gut-eater* were acceptable terms for Indians. (Eating animal guts was something only the uncivilized did, poor people and Indians, back in the days when buffalo roamed the plains.)

Indians who came to this town were lazy because instead of working they were paid by the federal government to go to the university.

Indians who stayed on the reservation were lazy because instead of working they were paid by the federal government to stay on the reservation.

I was a Jap. (Actually, this is not what the other kids called me, because by this time everyone knew that my father was Chinese. Rather, it was shouted out the window of pickup trucks as I walked along the sidewalk, waiting for the school bus, but since the trucks sped off, I could pretend that the drivers did not mean me, because of course I was not Japanese.)

11

My Last Confession

I thought I could make up for my sins by going to confession with my mother before Christmas. My mother loved everything to do with going to church, including confession. It was like a trip to the dentist, that same clean, sparkling feeling afterward, a shiny, unstained soul—until the next sin. I wanted that feeling again. I wanted to feel clean.

While my father and brother stayed at home, my mother drove us in her Jeep across the bumpy, snow-packed roads to the Newman Center. She was very happy. My mother's soul was always at peace when she went to church—or so it seemed to me, because she always smiled when we were together; I was not yet old enough for her to confide her fears in me—and she sang carols as she drove. I buried my chin in the folds of my scarf and rehearsed what I would tell the priest. The priests in New Jersey had explained to us all about just the kind of sins I was most guilty of: sins of omission, sins of cowardice, sins of complicity. I could picture Father McQuaid with his bright orange hair, speaking from the altar in his thick Irish brogue, his pale face growing scarlet as he flushed with outrage. Outrage and fear for our souls.

"There's no point in feeling proud of yourself if you've never committed a sin like murder or idol worship. If you've never stolen from a neighbor or coveted his wife. Maybe you've never had the opportunity," he said. He squinted at us from the altar, peering over his narrow reading glasses. Then he continued, his lips pursed, his expression curdling. "Instead, you should think about the sins you have committed. They might seem like lesser sins, times when you should have done the right thing but didn't, sins when you didn't do the Lord's work, sins that meant you looked the other way when your fellow man was in need."

These tiny sins could accumulate like dust specks, he explained, first a fine layer, almost invisible, and then, before you knew it, you were coated in sin.

I knew I was dusty indeed. And all because I had looked the other way when the Lord had called upon me to act: I hadn't spoken up in the face of prejudice. At first, I'd truly been too surprised to say anything. I was sitting in the lunchroom at my new middle school during a long, boring assembly, the kind where one of the P.E. teachers lectured us on personal hygiene or littering or fetal alcohol syndrome, something edifying. One of the girls who had befriended me leaned over and pointed to one of the Indian girls at another table.

"I can't stand her," she said, wrinkling her nose. "She thinks she's so great. But her family's just a bunch of welfare rats." Then she explained that their father got money from the government just to go to school, that's how they were able to buy such fancy clothes, never the same outfit twice, not for a whole month. Plus, the mother didn't work at all, had nothing better to do every morning than wrap her daughters' hair in rags so that the girls could have curls in time for school. My friend narrowed her eyes in disgust. "They make me sick," she said. I looked over at the Indian girls in their pretty flowered dresses and their dark curly hair, and said nothing.

Now the sin was on my soul, the same as if I'd said those hateful words myself. I tried to convince myself that I'd been too shocked to reply. I was no coward; I'd just been tongue tied. But why was my tongue so slow under some circumstances and not others?

When another girl at lunch had proclaimed confidently, "There's no such fruit as pineapple," I had not hesitated to argue with her, describing the pineapple plantations in Hawaii (which I'd never actually seen but whose existence I had surmised from the labels on cans of Dole pineapple). And when a friend of my brother's insisted that "sin made the lights go dim in bars," because that's what the pastor of his church had said, I wasted no time in explaining the nature of electricity and dimmer switches to him.

Yet when a grownup approached my mother while we were shopping in town—looking for new pants, as I was rapidly outgrowing all my clothes—I listened silently while she warned my mother to beware of the Indians in town.

"They can't be trusted. They hate us. I'm just letting you know for your own good," the woman insisted.

My mother laughed as though the woman were telling her a joke, as though the punch line were funny, and I thought I should support her; I should laugh, too, just as she did, a light, carefree warble, a brave laugh, a laugh that said we weren't worried at all. But when I tried to laugh my tongue seemed to swell within my dry mouth, my throat constricted. I could barely emit a cough.

"You don't know," the woman said to my mother again. The woman had followed us up to the cash register; she was standing close to my mother's elbow, her pointy boobs practically jutting into my mother's side. Out of the corner of my eye I saw my mother's hand ease into her purse and dig around for her key ring. When her hand emerged, the keys protruded between her fingers like claws.

The woman leaned closer. I could see her pores, the pale, dusty powder she wore on her skin, the odd way she'd shaved her eyebrows and drawn them in again in dark pencil. My mother's body stiffened. I put my hand against her thigh and could feel her muscles twitching beneath the fabric of her slacks. The keys jangled in her fist.

"We have to stick together," the woman whispered to my mother. "You have to know which side you're on."

The woman nodded twice and, satisfied that her message had been delivered, turned and walked out of the store, her cheap handbag perched delicately on her forearm.

"Well, wasn't she something else!" my mother exclaimed, turning back to the cashier. She laughed then, a sound so merry that other customers looked up to see what had happened. But the cashier didn't smile back.

I turned away and stared out the front windows of the store, which were already covered with a thick plastic sheet from the inside, protection from winter drafts. I pretended I didn't know that the other customers were staring at us. Outside the window I could see the wide main street, where the cars parked perpendicular to the curb in front of the funeral home and the Ben Franklin five-and-dime. I watched as the woman who had warned my mother crossed the street and then, recognizing a friend, smiled and waved happily, shaking her whole arm in the air, and another woman who looked just like her, the same pale ratted hair, covered with a net kerchief, the boxy slacks, the boxy coat, the boxy purse, waved back. When the woman smiled, she looked like a normal person, like anyone else.

I found my voice again only when I wrote letters home to my friends, ten pages, twelve pages, twenty-page assaults on our new town, my new school, my classmates. Here, in the security of my bedroom, I could speak again, but only at my favorite desk, the one with the top that rolled, the one I'd chosen from the Sears catalog the year before for Christmas. My writing desk. At my desk, I could compose both elegant and withering retorts, I could be both brave and witty. I could be bold like my father, I could laugh like my mother, and I could make people who said crazy, mean, frightening things hang their heads in shame. I was capable of fostering world peace at that desk.

But at school, when kids made jokes about Indians, when they used ugly words for other people's skin, when they laughed in a way that made my stomach fall to my knees, my wit and courage failed me, and I was silent.

The normally plain, stark brick interior of the church had been decorated for Christmas: colorful cloth banners hung from the rafters and poinsettias sat before the plaster statues of the saints in the alcoves on both sides of the wooden pews. On the altar itself, dozens of flower pots spilled down the steps, pooling on the carpet. It had been such a long time since I'd seen so much red. I felt surrounded by flame.

Overwhelmed, I knelt beside my mother and rested my forehead on my hands on the back of the pew in front of us. Other people seeing me might have mistaken my pose for piety, but I was simply reeling from all the color. By December the world had been bleached a snowy white. Snow covered every inch of our lives, two feet, three feet, collecting in the fields and the ditches, in the parking lots and on the roofs. Snow lay in drifts higher than cars. Snow blew across the streets and turned the asphalt white as bone. Snow flew in the wind and caught in my hair, clung to my eyelashes, burned against my cheeks, and slid unwelcomed down my throat with each gasp of air. Now I was back in a world filled with color; I felt faint.

Red reminded me of my grandmother. Nai-nai wore red vests over ancient silk *qipaos,* tied a gauzy persimmon-colored scarf around her neck, tucked scarlet embroidered handkerchiefs into her large black pocketbook. She couldn't stand being away from the color red, not even for a day.

Red reminded me of my grandfather, too. He gave me a red envelope every Christmas, every Chinese New Year, and every birthday, with a crisp new dollar bill inside to bring me luck. When our families gathered on the weekend at his favorite restaurant in Manhattan, he never forgot to order me a Shirley Temple with a bright red maraschino cherry speared on a plastic sword. When my father bragged to him that I'd made all A's in school, he told the waiter to bring me extra cherries. He always knew exactly what would make me smile.

I closed my eyes tightly, my blood pulsing red and maroon through the capillaries of my eyelids. I wasn't in church at all. I was at our Sunday dinner at Chun Cha Fu, with the deep vermilion walls and the gold double-happiness sign against a circle of crimson, the red neon welcome sign, the shiny round tables and the pomegranate cushions on the tall-backed chairs. I missed my uncles and aunt and cousins. I missed being part of a family, a family that no one stared at, a family that ate in our very own room in our favorite Chinese restaurant every Sunday.

I didn't want to open my eyes.

Now, when my grandparents called on the phone, they sounded so old. Their voices trembled, they forgot words, they repeated themselves. My grandfather had grown so deaf that he could no longer hear my voice very well. Sometimes when he called, if I picked up the phone first, he would continue to shout, "Hello? Hello?" and then, thinking the line had been cut, he'd hang up. My father shouted into the phone in Chinese when Ye-ye called, spittle flying, the sound bouncing off the walls, but my voice was too small.

My eyes still squeezed tightly shut, I was filled with hate for this place. My hatred boiled in my heart, turning my blood black, turning my stomach this way and that. I hated

the girl who said there was no such fruit as pineapple
the boys who used "Jew" as a verb
the girl who'd referred to my father as a Chinaman
the teacher who'd told everyone in my class that we'd moved here from China
my friends who made fun of Indians and black people, and myself for remaining silent because I was afraid they wouldn't be my friends if I spoke up
the vice president who'd lied to my mother about her job
the vice president who'd smiled tightly when my father talked about putting down roots
the men who'd called me a Jap out the windows of their pickup trucks
the men who'd shot at our house
the people who stared
the people who lived here
the Indians who didn't rise up and kill everyone else in their sleep the way people kept expecting them to
my father for bringing us here
my mother for being happy all the time anyway
my grandparents for growing old
my brother for staying small
me for growing up when I didn't want to
me for thinking hateful thoughts
me for being a coward
me

I balled my hands into fists, dug my nails into my palms until the pain grew so intense that I couldn't think of anything else, not my perfidious, fickle body that was changing so rapidly, not my grandparents, who were growing too old to protect any of us, not my hatred, which grew stronger every day. Only when my hands began to go numb did I dare open my eyes. I looked at my palms then just to admire the deep crescents cutting into my life lines.

My mother rose beside me to take her place in line for confession and I followed her obediently. The line divided in two, depending on whether you wanted to confess to the parish priest or the visiting priest. If you wanted to speak to our regular father, you went into the confessional, which was a box made of wood and no bigger than Dr. Who's phone booth. You could sit in shadow, your face obscured by the lattice-covered screen, but of course, if you'd gone to confession before, there was always the chance the priest might recognize your voice. It was a small congregation. If you wanted to confess to the visiting priest, there was no confessional at all. He sat in the open, off to the side of the altar, where you would kneel before him, face to face. The advantage of confessing to the visiting priest was that he didn't know any of us, but the disadvantage was clear.

I'd never had to make my confession without the safety of shadow, of anonymity, but now I told myself that I deserved the added humiliation and moved over to the shorter line that led to the visiting priest. Besides, I wanted to get it over with faster. I wanted to confess and be cleansed of my sins, and my terrible guilt. I wanted to feel free again.

As I waited in line, I rehearsed what I would say one last time. I would tell the priest not only about all of my silences, all of my complicity, but also about all the hatred inside me. So that I wouldn't get too nervous and freeze up, I reminded myself how wonderful I would feel when it was all over. I would be absolved of my sins, I wouldn't have to feel so guilty all the time, and with my fresh, clean soul I could be brave. I could find just the right words to keep my new friends but still make them stop saying terrible things that frightened me and worried me and stayed in my stomach so that late at night I could feel them bumping together in my guts as I lay awake, my hands on my abdomen, trying to push them back into silence.

By the time it was my turn to confess, I was ready. I knelt before the priest. I didn't try to hide my face, as other confessors had done. I didn't stare at the carpet. I didn't put my hands across my features, as though in prayer, as though my fingers could shield my sinning face from God. I lifted my face to him so that God could see me clearly through his eyes.

"Father, forgive me, for I have sinned," I began as I had been taught in second grade, and then calmly I poured out my heart to him.

When I was finished, I watched the priest's face anxiously for signs of shock or disgust, but in fact he merely looked a little bored.

"Well, well," he said, when he was certain that I had at last finished. I realized I had been rather verbose. After my months of silence, I had finally found the words to express my feelings.

"In order to be absolved of your sins of pride, you must say ten Our Fathers and three Hail Marys and pray the Lord God our Father to grant you humility," the priest said. He made the sign of the cross and told me that I would be forgiven if I followed his instructions, and then he sent me on my way back to the pews with a tired wave of his hand.

I staggered backward away from the altar. It seemed as though I had no feet. I couldn't feel them touching the carpet. I was floating down the center aisle of the church, tripping on my ankle bones, the air around me a blur of candlelight and stained glass while the red of the poinsettias steeped everything the color of tea. I did not feel light and free, as you're supposed to after confession, I did not feel cleansed: I felt whipped.

I had been hoping that he'd give me the name of the proper saint to pray to under my circumstances. The Italian kids back in New Jersey all seemed to know such things—pray to Saint Lucy for help on exams, Saint Christopher for protection on field trips, Saint Jude for lost causes. There was even rumored to be a saint who could help you get a date. But once again I had failed to use the right words. I should've asked the priest directly. I had been unclear. But no, I was just trying to console myself. The priest had understood me perfectly.

The priest's words clung to my skin like flies. "Sins of pride." "Pray for humility." Was there anything worse than this? I had never imagined such terrible things about myself. Arrogance. Sinful arrogance. We all knew only the meek inherited the earth. I was like the rich man who couldn't fit through the eye of a needle or enter the kingdom of heaven. I was like the Pharisees who cast the first stone. I was the worst kind of sinner. Any man might commit murder out of fear or rage, but pride and arrogance were something reserved for biblical villains like pharaohs and Roman soldiers.

I finally found an empty seat and slid to my knees. Automatically, I pressed my palms together before my face. They slid against each other, covered with sweat. I wiped them on the sides of my corduroy pants and tried again. I closed my eyes tightly and tried to pray. "Our Father, who art in heaven . . ." and then, "Hail Mary, full of grace . . ." I started and stopped. My hands were sweating too much. My heart was beating too fast. I slumped forward and laid my forehead against the cool wooden pew. I grasped the slick polished surface with all my fingers, as though for dear life, as though I were slipping from the earth, sliding off its round edges.

"Our Father . . ." "Hail Mary . . ." "Help, pray, give . . ."

The words couldn't come out. They were backing up in my throat. I was going to choke. Or worse, vomit.

With my eyes closed, the world was spinning too fast. I opened them and stared at the grain in the wood of the pew in front of me. I ran my fingers along the lines, tracing paths as though through a maze, as though I could find a line that would straighten and lead me to safety.

I had been right. I was a sinner. It was all my fault. I was going to hell.

My mother finished her confession and found me in the pews. She looked refreshed, happy, the same as always. She knelt and prayed beside me.

I thought over my options. If God was going to forgive me, I would have to say my Hail Marys and my Our Fathers and I would have to ask him to grant me humility. The priest had said so. It must be true.

But as I knelt slumped in my pew, tracing the wood with my fingertips, I knew I couldn't do it. I couldn't pray for humility. I was too frightened that God might grant my request. And although I knew it meant I might go to hell, really and truly and for eternity, I could not pray for something I did not want. I could not pray for something that I knew would not help me survive here.

I realized then that I had made my last confession. I would never go again.

12 Bugs

As if winter hadn't been bad enough, spring arrived. All at once the snow melted and the fields turned to mud. Thick, stinky, sticky mud that coated my shoes like red paint, that splattered from the tires, that ran like a river through the ditches and the gutters and puddled on the sidewalks. Everywhere mud.

My father began to complain constantly. I think he had imagined living in the country like a Confucian scholar. Occasionally he might look up from his books and, from the comfort of his study, stare out the window and contemplate nature. He had not imagined that nature would insist upon our full attention.

Tornadoes arrived with the rains. Sirens wailed in town and soon our neighbors were camped out in our basement, their boys running through our house, tracking the mud across the cream-colored carpets, my mother and me forced to cook for hours just to feed everyone. Our neighbors always bragged that they'd lived here for five generations but had never bothered to build a storm cellar. Now they were in our house. Once, in a panic, one of their sons parked his pickup not in our driveway but in the middle of the lawn. After the storm passed, we discovered the truck had sunk into the sod. The boy spun the tires, trying to extricate the truck, leaving deep trenches that filled quickly with mud. My father was furious. After they left, he yelled at us, my mother and brother and me, as though we had deliberately caused the tornado, as though we were throwing a secret party that he'd stumbled upon. Every time he looked out the window, that's all he could see. Not the perfect expanse of his green country lawn, but two foot-deep pits, like a latrine in the middle of his scholar's garden. Later, my mother convinced the neighbors to fill in the pits with sod. Another time, the neighbors broke our wood-burning stove in the basement. Having grown bored waiting for the all-clear signal, they'd decided to disassemble it, only to discover that they had no idea how to put it back together again. All this happened while my mother cooked pancakes upstairs. Soon, every time the tornado sirens came screeching to life, my father became doubly agitated, not so much about the danger of being blown away to Oz as about the invasion of neighbors and what they'd do to our property. The tornados came spinning overhead all spring.

Then, just as the weather warmed up, as the sun returned and dried up all that mud, came the bugs. Some days, in a rage, my father would charge outdoors wielding a fly swatter in each hand and bat at the air, whirling around and around, his arms in constant motion until he'd worked up a sweat, his shirt drenched, his face burning to the touch.

"Come inside, Winberg," my mother called to him. Only she could get him to give up swatting flies outdoors. She'd help him out of his sweaty clothes and force him into the shower, while my brother and I hid in our rooms or downstairs under the ping-pong table. Our father tended to have a terrible temper when he was in his bug-killing mode and we wanted to stay clear; otherwise he'd hand us the swatters and order us outside to finish the job.

The bugs were like a biblical plague. They hopped out of the fields at us, they dropped from the trees, crickets and grasshoppers and ticks and strange, stick-like insects I'd never imagined existed. They stung, they bit, they burrowed under our skin. They clung to our clothes. They rode into our house on our backs and chirped from the corners of the closets. Miasmas of biting gnats rose from the fields at dusk. Mosquitoes hovered in the ditches like a bad dream. A farmer to the west raised bees, of all things, and escapees fled the artificial hives to nest around our house.

In desperation, my father ordered a special "bug-zapping" lamp he'd seen in a catalog and installed it in front of the garage. Its pale blue light was supposed to attract insects into its heated inner coils and then "zap" them to death. As advertised, it attracted bugs all right. Every bug from every field for miles around. In the country night, our bug lamp was the brightest light around, and the bugs responded as though making a religious pilgrimage. All night long I could hear the bug lamp zap-zap-zapping away. I rose from my bed at one point and watched from the front window as the blue light flashed and another bug's body burst into flame, again and again. The next morning, our driveway and lawn were littered with dead insects, large ebony beetles flipped onto the backs of their charred shells, red-and-black box elder bugs scattered like pistachio shells, and unidentifiable insects that seemed to have arrived from a Hitchcock film. My brother and I swept up the bodies and put them into Hefty bags for the trash men to take away before our father, the city boy, could see them and throw another fit. Everywhere we stepped, our feet crunched their bodies. I imagined that I could feel their crisp skeletons through the soles of my shoes.

The only bugs that avoided the lamp of death were the ones he hated most of all, the mosquitoes and biting gnats and flies—enormous horse-shit-eating flies, blue-black bottle flies, houseflies.

I thought that if it hadn't been for all those bugs, perhaps everything would have turned out differently. There was only so much a man like my father could take. This kind of thinking was the only way at age twelve I could make sense of what happened next.

In May, just a few weeks before my thirteenth birthday, my father came home early one afternoon. My brother and I had just arrived home from school. We hadn't expected our father for hours yet. We'd been setting up dominoes in the living room, where we were forbidden to play as my father always wanted one room of the house to be "presentable," although his idea of presentable seemed to matter less and less here. Now his Buick was barreling down the gravel road. Hurriedly, we swept the dominoes off the table and into our arms, into the bottoms of our shirts, stuffed strays into the pockets of our jeans, and then took off running down the hall to our bedrooms where we could dump our dominoes onto the floor and shut the door in a flash.

I sat with my ear to the door, so that I could eavesdrop on my parents.

I heard my father come inside and my mother greet him in the kitchen. Then suddenly there was a strange, atypical silence. My parents were both talkers, and sometimes they talked at the same time. There was no such thing as silence when they were in a room together.

Curious, I crept into the hallway where I could hear better.

And then I heard my father tell my mother that he had resigned.

My mother was shocked. He hadn't consulted her first. My father explained that he hadn't planned it either. There had been a meeting with the president that afternoon. The other vice presidents were there. My father had wanted to clear the air. He admitted that he'd been unhappy. There was so much resistance to all that he'd wanted to accomplish. All his plans. How could he, as vice president for academic affairs, have any kind of impact if all of his suggestions went nowhere? He said that he didn't think it was working out. And, to his surprise, they agreed with him.

He'd signed all the papers in the president's office, he told my mother. At first he'd thought about keeping his tenured teaching position in the political science department, just as a safety net, but the other administrators had said, no, that wasn't possible, and so he'd resigned everything at once. He agreed to stay on one additional year for the president's sake, to work on a transition, but then he'd be free to leave.

"Oh, Winberg," my mother gasped.

My father shook his head. "It wasn't working out," he said. "If I hadn't resigned, they would have asked me to leave or they would have made it impossible for me to function."

He sat down then at the kitchen counter, his arms hanging limply from his sides.

"We'll sell the house. I'll get another job. We can move anywhere you want," he said.

My mother put her head in her hands and cried.

I remember the quality of light that afternoon when I stumbled upon my parents talking in low voices in the kitchen. Everything was shimmering in the spring sunlight, rays poured in all the windows of our house, bleaching the color from the carpet and walls. I held my hands up in the light, palms open, and my skin seemed to glow. Everything was buzzing, the cicadas in the trees hummed louder and louder, the clock on the wall ticked away; I could hear the gears turning behind the second hand. Suddenly I was aware of my heart beating within my ribcage, the sound vibrating through my bones.

I watched as my father put his arm around my mother's shoulders. They both trembled.

13

The Fall of the Prince

That June, my father left for Harvard to attend a summer institute for university administrators, as he'd originally planned to do before his resignation, and the rest of us stayed on the farm. At first, we were all optimistic. My mother was confident that my father would find a new job soon, and this time, he promised, it would be in a warmer climate.

I was close to ecstatic. We would be leaving, I knew, in one year's time. Suddenly my perspective changed. I no longer dreaded each new day. Instead I felt as though I were a journalist or anthropologist studying the ways of a newly discovered exotic land. I kept copious notes in my diary. Everything seemed curious and important—the menu at the bowling alley/steakhouse, the way the high school kids cruised up and down the three blocks of the downtown in the evening, circling round and round, revving engines and calling to each other from the windows of their pickups. I tried to pick up the local accent—an interesting short "u" sound that fell somewhere between the "oo" in root and the "u" in rut; the flat, nasal "a"; the slight upturn in the middle of sentences rather than at the end. Creek was pronounced "crick," wrestling, "wrassling." Unfortunately, at age thirteen, my tongue was not very flexible, and whereas my brother soon sounded like a native, I could not. I also recorded the differences in vocabulary I had noted thus far. For example, lunch meant a sweet, midday snack. The noon meal was called dinner, the evening meal, supper. There was no such drink as soda; instead everyone referred to pop. When I tried using a different word for any of these, such as calling a Coke a soda, I was met with blank stares. This situation had driven me nuts in the beginning, but now I found it merely curious.

Naturally, I also kept lists of all the unique ethnic slurs I had picked up. Someday this type of knowledge might come in handy. Who knew?

My mother was determined that we should have our farm experience before we left, so she bought two Nubian goats, which I named Erma Bombeck and Madeleine L'Engle. My brother was allowed to start a flock of ducks and geese. She also bought two puppies from a farmer who assured us that they would be good around other animals. They were jet black with brown, mask-like markings around their eyes. At first they were heavy, slow-moving creatures. We were barely able to lift them and they spent most of the day dozing in the shade. Within weeks they ballooned in size, like small buffalo, and learned to bark whenever anyone drove up to our house, including us. They didn't seem particularly bright, but they were loyal. My brother and I named them Bert and Ernestine in honor of the Muppets.

Finally, my mother decided we should have a barn. What good was a farm without one? And she figured it would increase the value of the property. She drew up the designs, hired a local carpenter, and my brother spent his summer learning to build, helping the man dig the foundation, pour and spread the concrete, and even shingle the roof. When it was finished, we painted the whole thing a deep brick red.

"Isn't our farm beautiful?" my mother proclaimed with satisfaction.

Even I had to agree that it was.

When my father returned in August, he was surprised to find all the animals. But my mother convinced him that what's fair is fair. She had wanted a farm. Besides, if he could resign from a job without consulting her first, surely she could buy a few animals.

He put up a fuss in the beginning, claiming he could smell the stinky geese even from inside the house. And our dogs—we now had four—ate tremendous amounts of food. But after Bert and his sister began barking ferociously every time someone drove by our house, scaring unknown visitors away, running right up to the tires when people slowed their pickups, my father came to like the dogs.

"My father always had a watchdog in China," he said. "To guard against thieves. I don't mind dogs if they earn their keep."

Now, at night, when I lay in my bedroom with the windows open, I could hear our dogs running around the house in a pack (although my little dog, Betty, was allowed to sleep in the laundry room). I could hear them panting and snorting, sneezing and wheezing, as they ran in circles, faster and faster, chasing invisible prey. They sometimes ran into the fields beside our property but they always returned quickly. If a car or truck approached, they barked and howled protectively, long before the vehicle was anywhere near our house.

I no longer felt afraid when I went to bed at night. I felt our dogs would keep us safe.

That fall, everyone at school seemed to know already what had happened at the university with my father's job. They kept asking where we would move next. I shrugged easily. "To the coast, I think," which sounded exotic and pleasing to me.

In October, Ye-ye and Nai-nai came to visit. They wanted to see the farm before we left. But when they arrived one blustery day, nothing about our reunion turned out as I'd expected.

My parents had dropped them off at my middle school after picking them up at the airport. I was reading in social studies, when suddenly I heard my classmates twittering around me. I looked up and, to my surprise, Ye-ye and Nai-nai were standing in front of the book stacks, waving at me.

My teacher allowed me to get up and show them around the school. I hurried from my seat and led my grandparents away. I didn't want my classmates' poisonous stares to fall upon their shoulders. I felt I needed to protect them, but perhaps I only made my grandparents feel rushed. They seemed so small to me now, so fragile, not at all the way I remembered. I had been growing so rapidly, I now towered over my grandfather. And my grandmother, always so strong and robust in New Jersey, had trouble walking, her hips were hurting, and she leaned heavily against my arm.

My grandparents weren't actually interested in the school, but I led them to the library and then back toward the lunchroom where there was a display of artwork in a glass case. I pointed to a clay mouse I had made. They pretended to look at it, then leaned their heads together and muttered in Chinese. Finally, Ye-ye translated for me, smiling broadly. "Oh, Mei-mei," he called me by my childhood nickname. "You're so tall now! We don't recognize you!" Then he and my grandmother laughed.

I frowned. That was the last thing I wanted to hear. I wanted everything to be the same as before, back when we'd seen each other every weekend, when I was little and they were giants.

Later, at our house, my grandparents immediately went to the guest room to take a long nap. They were tired after their journey across the country. There were no direct flights from New York in those days; they'd had to change planes in Minneapolis and again in Des Moines. My parents had picked them up in Sioux City, Iowa, and driven them the final forty miles to our town. They slept for quite a while. I could hear their gentle snores from my perch on the stairs outside their door.

After Ye-ye and Nai-nai had finished napping, my brother wanted to show them his snow geese, which had matured into a beautiful flock. The geese were quite hostile to me, hissing and squawking and flapping their enormous wings every time I approached their pen, but they loved my brother and followed him around in a line, honking politely for food.

My grandfather rubbed his hands together happily as he observed the geese. He turned to my father. "Winberg, let me kill one tonight. I know the best recipe for snow goose."

Ye-ye was speaking in Chinese, so fortunately my brother couldn't understand, but I knew something was wrong by the way my father immediately shook his head and his hands and then spoke rapidly to my grandfather in Mandarin. Ye-ye then started, his eyebrows jumping. He looked at the geese and laughed.

"Pets!" he said in English, shaking his head, as though he couldn't believe it.

For the next week, my parents tried to keep my grandparents occupied, driving them around town to visit the campus, the tiny museum with the display of the stuffed buffalo and Indian arrowheads, even the bowling alley/steakhouse. I couldn't tell what my grandparents thought. They didn't speak much in the back of the car but seemed to have sunk into the upholstery. When we returned home my father had to help them out of the car, taking them by the hands and pulling.

When the men came by shooting on the weekend, they were naturally alarmed.

"Just hunters, just hunters," my father said, waving a hand airily, as though he were a British squire talking about a weekend fox hunt.

Before long, my grandmother started dispensing advice again. She wrote long notes for my father and placed them at his spot at the kitchen table, anchored with a teacup or the stapler so there'd be no chance they would blow away and be lost.

Sitting in our dining room, Nai-nai shook her head anxiously, watching me as I did my homework. She told my mother to be careful. To dress me in plain clothes. "Don't let her wear makeup. Don't let her curl her hair." She seemed to think I was reaching a dangerous age.

Just before they left, we posed for pictures. When I wrapped my arm around my grandfather's shoulders, I could feel his bones poking through his suit jacket. When my grandmother leaned against my arm, I could feel her panting heavily, her chest heaving. In the final photograph, it's just the two of them, standing side by side in our driveway before our house, the fields extending to the horizon behind them. My grandfather wears a black beret with a jaunty stem. My grandmother is wearing her curly wig, with a red, gauzy scarf tied under her chin. They appear so small under the big sky, heavy with clouds. They are clinging to each other, as though the wind might blow them away, across the empty fields, over the bone-like cornstalks broken from harvesting and into the endless sky, like a pair of paper grandparents, fragile as kites. They cling to each other, arm in arm, as though they're afraid they might never make it back to New York.

That April, Nai-nai died in her sleep.

One morning as my father was preparing to leave for work, Ye-ye called and said that my grandmother was dead. She had never awakened that morning. He'd found the body, cold in her bed, when he'd gone into her bedroom to see what she wanted for breakfast.

My father grew very still. He held the phone so tightly in his hand, his knuckles shone through his skin. Later, he'd say he couldn't believe it. She'd seemed healthy enough when they'd visited. She'd been writing him long letters every week with advice, how to deal with the other administrators, places to look for new jobs, ways to make friends with farmers she'd learned from her experience in China's villages during World War II, offers to send mothballs to combat the insects. She assured him that the mothballs in Chinatown were better, stronger than the ordinary American kind. They didn't just repel moths but also cockroaches and flies. She wanted to know how many packages he wanted. Were these the words of a dying woman?

My father went to work that morning and returned home for lunch, then went back to work. He acted as though everything were normal except that his face was too pale, his shoulders seemed too heavy for his skeleton, and his voice was quiet. For the first time in my life, the sound barely crawled from his throat.

It was up to my mother to make the travel arrangements for him, buy the airline tickets, call my grandfather and uncles and tell them when my father would arrive. She wrote his eulogy too, the one he was supposed to deliver at the funeral, and put together a booklet about my grandmother's life, important dates, a few black-and-white photos from her youth, a couple of psalms. She persuaded the local printer to make it a rush job.

Then, in the days before the funeral, Ye-ye called with reports of sightings of my grandmother. She had appeared in a dream of his, displeased and scowling. She had appeared to my middle uncle at the end of the hallway while he was awake. She'd told him they'd wasted their lives, saving their money like refugees, hoarding paper bags and napkins and condiments "borrowed" from the neighborhood McDonald's, filling their apartment with trash she'd refused to throw away. It had all been her idea, this thrift, but now she was back to say that she'd been wrong. My uncle promised her that he'd do better by his father, and the very next day he cashed in his stocks and bought my grandfather a brand-new convertible. Pink. My grandfather made him take it back immediately, without even going for a spin around the block. Finally, Ye-ye reported that Nai-nai had appeared at the end of his bed, speaking words he could not understand. He cried on the phone, and my father tried to console him; I heard him say, over and over, "You were a good husband, you were a good husband," in Chinese and English.

For my part, I grew frightened, wondering when my grandmother would show up here as well. I grew self-conscious when I dressed and undressed, aware of my new breasts, my growing hips, all that hair everywhere. Once, feeling goose bumps prickle up and down my arms as I showered, I was convinced that my grandmother was watching me from heaven. I could almost feel her flickering in the bathroom, hovering by the mirror, waiting for me with her lips pursed, ready to pronounce me in some way unfit, to warn me of my failings. In my experience, Nai-nai was happiest when she could predict calamity. In this way she had kept the family moving during World War II, never complacent, always vigilant. This skill had saved lives in China, but in America her talent had seemed merely disheartening.

Quickly, I opened the shower doors and thrust my hand out. I patted the wall frantically, searching for the light switch without daring to stick my head out and possibly catch a glimpse of my commanding grandmother's ghost. Finally, I was able to turn off the light. I felt safer then, as though in the dark we were both invisible. I finished washing—and dressing—without turning the light back on.

But later, lying awake in my bed, safely dressed in pajamas, listening to the wind blowing through the trees and the horses snorting in the field next door and our dogs running circles around the house in the moonlight, I felt braver, and I tried to call to Nai-nai with my thoughts. I worried that I had chased her away, botched the last opportunity I would have ever to see her again. I wanted her to appear to me as she had to my uncle, or at the very least to visit my dreams with a message just for me. I waited, staring into the dark, but she never came.

When my father went back to New York for the funeral, he called my mother every night to tell her about the horrors of his days, of comforting his father, who continued to weep publicly, of the strangeness he felt when gazing upon his mother's body in her coffin. He hadn't recognized her at first. Her corpse was wearing too much makeup, he said. How could this have been his mother?

When my father returned, he looked different. He was still the same person, the same bushy eyebrows, the wiry black hair, the lips pressed together in a straight determined line, but there was something unusual about his appearance, too. At first I couldn't quite place it. It was more a feeling than a physical trait that had changed, I decided. So long as my grandmother had been alive, he would always be her first-born son, the family prince, and he'd carried himself as though he wore an invisible gold crown on his head. If he slumped just a little, it might fall off. Now, when he came home from work, he carried himself in a different manner. He didn't act like a prince returning to his castle, but returned like a man who was merely tired after a long day.

Honeymoon at Niagara Falls: *(left to right)* Winberg, Carolyn, and Winberg's parents, Nai-nai and Ye-ye.

Winberg, baby May-lee, and Carolyn in front of their home in Redlands, California, 1967.

Ye-ye, baby May-lee, and Nai-nai in the backyard, Redlands, California, 1967.

Jeff and May-lee, circa 1970.

May-lee, Carolyn, and Jeff at a political rally in Chinatown, New York City, circa 1975.

Winberg, May-lee, Jeff, and Carolyn at home in New Jersey, circa 1978.

The family on their farm in South Dakota, fall 1980: *(left to right)* Jeff, Bert the dog, Winberg, May-lee, Betty the dog, Carolyn, and the goats Erma Bombeck and Madeleine L'Engle.

Jeff and May-lee with three of their dogs, 1980.

Carolyn and Winberg, glamour couple, 1981.

May-lee, age seventeen, and her pig pose for May-lee's high school yearbook senior picture, fall 1984.

The family poses in the backyard of their Wyoming home, circa 1990.

The family in Laramie, Wyoming, 2005: *(left to right)* Winberg; Jeff's daughter, Ariel; May-lee with Suki the dog; Jeff's wife, Virginia; Jeff's son, Everett; Jeff; and Jeff's younger daughter, Adelaide.

14

The Jade Tree

We packed up the entire house the summer I turned fourteen, preparing to leave as soon as one of my parents had a firm job offer. My father had several leads in Oregon and Texas, and my mother had an interview in California. My parents were nervous, they jumped at loud noises, they lost their tempers easily, they grew quite thin and yet still refused to eat supper, picking at the food with their forks.

For his part, my brother cried when he thought about leaving all his animals, which now included two Holsteins. He knew there was no way he'd be able to keep so many animals when we moved, and he grew depressed and surly. He didn't want to help pack up our things and spent most of the summer with the goats and the ducks and the geese and the dogs and the cows, or else rearranging the metal trash cans in which we kept the animal's feed in the barn.

I, on the other hand, couldn't wait to move. Sometimes I felt disloyal to be so happy while everyone else in my family was depressed—sometimes, but not very often. I wrote long, florid letters to my friends in New Jersey at my writer's roll-top desk, sending Polaroids I'd taken of the mounting stacks of packed boxes. Progress reports, I called them.

Some time that summer some of the girls I knew from middle school called to say they were going to throw a going-away party for me and another girl who was moving. It would be our last time to see each other, probably in our lives, the invitation said: would I come? The whole party was probably one of their mothers' ideas. We weren't particularly close, these girls and I, we had had a few classes together at most, and today I can't even remember the name of the other girl who was moving. But I agreed to go to the party. One last entry for my anthropologist's diary, I figured. One of the mothers volunteered to drive us to and from the roller rink in Yankton, twenty-eight miles away.

My parents were worried about letting me attend, as we hadn't had very good experiences in Yankton, a town of ten thousand. Yankton had a small mall, anchored by a Sears and a farm implements store. It had a McDonald's—the only one in our corner of the state. And, inexplicably to us, it had a medical clinic that was renowned for having Jewish doctors.

We'd checked out Yankton our first year there. We'd seen an ad for a Chinese restaurant in the yellow pages and my father had to try it. This was before he'd given up entirely on the Chinese food in the region. We'd gone to the mall first and walked around, only to find that there weren't many stores. The farm economy was hurting and many chains had pulled out. Windows were soaped up and dark, with no replacement businesses scheduled to move in. In the parking lot a man in a plaid, western-style shirt, the kind with snaps, and a John Deere cap, stepped up to us in the parking lot and hissed, "Chinks!"

Turning to us, my father remarked loudly that he was impressed. The people in *our* town mistakenly called us "Japs"! We laughed, and the man looked startled, turned red, and hurried away, scuttling in a bowlegged fashion to his truck.

We finally found the Chinese restaurant after driving up and down the broad, tree-lined streets of nearly identical houses on very small plots of lawn. I couldn't understand why the towns in this part of the country were so congested, the houses so close together, when there was so much land just outside the town limits. The houses appeared to huddle anxiously, as if afraid of the enormous sky. (I didn't understand because I hadn't yet experienced a Dakota winter.)

The restaurant was a tiny, dingy affair, no bigger than someone's garage in New Jersey. It had a terrible name, some kind of bad joke, like the Yank-Ton Won-Ton. Someone had thrown a rock through the sign, which at one point must have lighted up but now was dark and wounded, with a hole just below the last "Ton." The parking lot had space for about four cars and was completely empty.

It wasn't a promising sight, to be sure, but my father was desperate.

"Sometimes these little hole-in-the-wall places are the best," he said hopefully. "More authentic."

"I can remember some of the wonderful tacquerias in Mexico City. Just a tiny stand, but such delicious food," my mother added. She understood how important it was for my father to have hope.

Inside, it was so dark we had to stand completely still, clustered by the door, blinking, for long seconds before our eyes adjusted and we could safely walk into the cramped interior without fear of tripping. There were a few tables in the middle of the place, and in the corner a lone booth, which was occupied by a rather elderly Chinese woman. She sat slumped across the table, her chin on her fist, and didn't move even when my father called out to her. She was the most depressed-looking person I had ever seen in my life.

(A few years later, when I myself would become the most depressed-looking person I had ever seen, the image of this woman would come back to haunt me. I would understand exactly what was going through her mind. It was the same thing that was going through mine: that I had died and gone to hell.)

After a few minutes, a perky white girl emerged from the kitchen and told us to sit anywhere we wanted. She handed us menus on which every item was preceded by a number. Everything came with a side of fried rice and an egg roll. I suggested we leave and go to McDonald's before it was too late, but my father had become pathologically obsessed with eating the Yank-Ton Won-Ton's food. "We're here, we're here," he repeated unnecessarily. "Eat, eat." It was like some kind of medieval religious devotion, the kind with hair shirts and self-flagellation with pronged leather whips, my father's need to try every Chinese restaurant we could find.

The food came, and everything was served on individual plates that had partitions like our middle school cafeteria trays. Every dish was the color beige. My father ate his entire plate of food in one long, continuous munching motion, his fork shoveling beige fried rice and beige meat chunks with beige peanuts into his mouth. He ate practically without chewing, as though that would lessen the pain. He ate as though the idea of eating Chinese food were more important than the reality. Then he drank six cups of tea, trying to wash the flavor from his mouth.

"I feel sick," he announced. "I think it's food poisoning."

"Oh, Winberg, why did you eat all that?" my mother sighed.

"I couldn't help myself." He scraped his tongue with his paper napkin.

"Stop that!" My mother glanced over her shoulder, embarrassed, but the white girl had disappeared and the old Chinese lady hadn't moved.

"I didn't want to eat it! You shouldn't have made me come here!" My father tried to pour himself another cup of tea but the pot was empty.

We were all in a bad mood by the time we drove home.

Because of our previous disappointments with Yankton, my parents weren't thrilled about my going to the roller-skating party, but they finally let me go after one of the girls' mothers called and assured them we would be chaperoned and that she would personally drive each of us home.

I don't remember the particulars of the going-away party. I'm pretty sure we ate bad roller-rink pizza and drank too many sugary soft drinks and circled around the rink to the strains of Rick Springfield and Wham, who were popular that year.

I remember that one girl, Kitty, expressed mock sympathy that I was leaving. "You're like a tumbleweed. You don't have any roots," she said, squinting at me. In fact, it had been her idea to throw this party, I discovered. She obviously seemed to think there was some shame in moving. "We're like the crops," she said proudly. "We grow here."

"A rolling stone gathers no moss," I retorted.

Kitty didn't like that very much and rolled away to talk to somebody else.

By nine-thirty, Kitty's mother said it was time to go, and I remember the giddy feeling that settled in my chest, my heart thumping faster and faster. My going-away party was over. It was only a matter of time now and I'd truly be gone.

Some of the girls began to sniffle sentimentally. They promised to keep in touch. They said how much they would miss me and the other girl who was leaving. I probably lied and said something like that, too. We girls learn to dissemble early.

Then we climbed into Kitty's mother's station wagon and began the long drive home. All the girls lived in the countryside like me, and that meant we had to take ten-, twelve-, fourteen-mile detours off the state highway to find their farms then drive back to the highway until we reached the next country road.

By the time we reached my house it was well after midnight. I could see my father pacing in the golden light of our front window. Just from his posture, his hunched shoulders, the agitated way he swung his arms, the syncopated rhythm of his steps, I knew something was wrong.

Uh oh, I thought. At a glance I could tell he was furious.

As I came in the front door, I could hear my mother's voice, "Now calm down, hush, everything's all right." I realized she was talking to my father. He was still pacing by the window, as though I hadn't come in at all; he looked out into the black night and muttered something under his breath. Everything felt wrong. The air was charged, as though I'd just missed a lightning strike. And then I saw it. The jade tree, lying in pieces on the carpet.

I gasped.

"Your father just got a little upset," my mother began. "He was beginning to worry—"

"Where were you?" my father exploded. "You were supposed to be here by ten-thirty!"

"Kitty's mother had to drive everybody home. We left at nine-thirty. We've been driving around all this time." I took off my shoes and walked over to the corner of the living room to examine the poor jade tree. I knelt down to examine a broken blossom. "Oh, no! The perfect one! You broke the perfect one! How could you?"

My father was beginning to calm down. He was still pacing, but no longer with the intensity of a tiger in a cage. He paced as though he didn't know where to go.

"I don't know why I did it," he said finally, his voice small and thin, as though he were just beginning to grasp the enormity of what he'd done.

My mother stood with her arms folded across her chest. Now that she no longer had to try to calm my father, her voice acquired an angry edge. "He just couldn't control himself. Not ten minutes before you came home, and this is what he does. I told him you were a good girl. You know how to handle yourself. You were coming home—"

I couldn't believe my crazy parents, the odd way they were talking, as though I'd been out on a date. As though I were somehow disobeying them, flouting their authority, when they knew all along I was going to some dorky roller-skating party with a bunch of other girls. I felt like a character on a surrealist sitcom. "I didn't have any choice, Ma!" I shouted. "Kitty's mother was driving us all home! What could I do? I couldn't come home by myself!"

"Hush, don't shout," my mother said and went into the kitchen. She was tired and she didn't need my anger on top of my father's.

I knelt on the floor and began picking up the jade petals. I was going to throw up. I was going to cry. I didn't want my father to see me lose control, and so I bent over the sliver of jade in my hand as though I were examining it very closely. I had loved our jade tree ever since I was a child. It was not, in fact, entirely made of jade. The trunk and limbs of the foot-high tree were made from a twisted wiry metal and then coated with layers of dark cloth that was treated with a chemical in such a way that it resembled bark. It was set in an octagonal cloisonné base, which had darkened with age so that the ornate pattern of geometrically abstract peonies was nearly invisible. I used to trace the pattern with my finger, as though I were reading an ancient form of Braille.

The most beautiful parts of the jade tree were the blossoms. Rather than imitate any kind of plant found in nature, the artists who had created our tree endowed it with magical qualities, so that all the flowers of paradise bloomed on its branches: dogwood and plum blossoms made from translucent white jade, pale green chrysanthemums, lavender peonies, and lush pink litchi made of a quartz that seemed to glow from within. Each leaf was fashioned from the darkest green jade, carved and polished till it shone. Each blossom was fastened to its branch with a metal collar, shaped like a stamen, and a few wires twisted into an elegant knot. Now the blossoms lay broken on the floor, snapped from the branches, their wires exposed like so many dangling nerves.

Some of my earliest memories were of my father lovingly dusting the jade tree. When we lived in California, every month my father would take the jade tree down from its perch beside our bust of Guan Yin, the Goddess of Mercy, and set it on the low lacquer coffee table before our living room couch. Next he set a box of Q-Tips and a can of Pledge to one side, and then, wearing white cotton gloves, he would spray one Q-Tip with a little Pledge and begin the slow process of dusting the tree, petal by petal, leaf by leaf. When I was very little, he refused to allow me to so much as touch the tree, and I had to sit four feet away on the floor while he cleaned it. He took off his glasses for the close work, pressing his nose so close to each flower that I was convinced he was sniffing them. Later, after he had put the tree back on its stand and left the room, I would stealthily climb up on a chair and lean into the jade tree to see if I could smell the blossoms, too. I discovered that they smelled sweet and vaguely of Pledge.

The first time my father let me dust the tree I was five, in kindergarten, and he gave me a set of my very own Q-Tips and allowed me to wipe the leaves. I couldn't have been more proud. However, that particular jade tree, our first, was bent and missing several blossoms. It listed to one side. Its twin, the perfect, undamaged one, resided in my grandparents' apartment in New York. They'd brought both jade trees all the way from China. Just before the Japanese had invaded Nanjing, they'd buried them in the backyard, deep in holes that the servants dug in the middle of the night so the neighbors wouldn't see. After the war the family had returned to their house and dug up the trees. That's when they discovered that the one tree had been damaged. It was a shame, but my grandmother refused to part with the trees, even when they needed to sell everything of value just to buy food during the period of hyperinflation after the war. She'd sell her jewelry, she'd sell off chunks of her inheritance from her mother, bit by bit, but she wouldn't sell the jade trees.

In 1949, when the Communists were clearly going to win the civil war against the Nationalists, my grandparents took the trees with them when they fled Nanjing with my father and his brothers. They had to be practical. They had to leave most everything behind. They knew if they were going to make it out alive before the People's Liberation Army took over Nanjing, the capital, they would have to travel light. Yet they couldn't bear to part with the jade trees.

My grandparents carried them to Shanghai and Guangzhou and Taiwan and finally New York. When my father moved away from his parents to take his first tenure-track job in California, my grandparents had given him two gifts for luck. One was the Goddess of Mercy statue. The other was the listing jade tree.

Then, just before we left New Jersey, Ye-ye gave us its twin, the perfect tree, the one that had survived two wars and two ocean journeys intact. He wanted us to have the matching set. We should remember, Ye-ye said, this was a lucky tree.

Now it lay in pieces, even more broken than the first one.

My father joined me on the carpet, squatting on his heels, searching for pieces of jade, patting the floor with both hands.

What I did not know, what I could not understand on the night of my going-away party, was that I had ceased to be a child. From now on my life at home would be different from all the previous days and nights of my life, as my parents became increasingly fraught with anxiety about my well-being, expressing that anxiety in dramatic and, to my mind, illogical ways.

My father would accuse me of wanting to marry some farmer's son, and then he'd name the most disgusting boy he could think of, like the kid who picked his nose when he ate or the boy who never washed his hair.

"You're going to marry him and live here forever!" he shouted at me.

When he talked like this, I felt as though I were completely naked and bugs were crawling all over my skin, bugs that everyone could see but me, bugs that exuded a bad smell. I wanted to run and hide. But instead I shouted, "I'm never getting married! I wouldn't want to be married for anything in the world!"

But still my father would not be placated. While he bought my brother a three-wheeler, a four-wheeler, a pickup, a motorcycle, and finally a red Honda Civic over the years, I was obliged to walk to school and to work or to hitch a ride with my brother. My father hid the keys of his Buick from me. He was being a typical Chinese father for his generation and class, protecting his daughter from what he considered a fate worse than death—a date with a peasant's son—but for years it made me hate him, the fact that he didn't trust me, the fact that he knew nothing about my tastes.

15 The Nights of Many Prayers

By midsummer we'd packed up everything in the house and decided to move to northern California, where my mother had a job interview. My father had not as yet had any firm job offers, but he was not yet panicked. My mother was feeling a little nervous about her interview, which would represent her first full-time return to the job market since my brother and I were born, but my father encouraged her, reminding her of the powerful career she'd built before they were married. She was still young and good-looking—"Beautiful!" he said. "Like a movie star!" She had nothing to worry about.

After months of showing the house to what seemed like everyone in town—even professors who claimed they were interested in buying but we later discovered never intended to leave their own houses—we finally found a buyer. It had been awful, the selling process. The real estate agents made us leave the house for hours on end while they showed it, and in a town our size there were very few places to go. We ended up spending a lot of time washing all the blankets and comforters at the Laundromat. We'd return home to find the drawers of our dressers pulled out, our clothes rifled through. Boxes of food were removed from our kitchen cabinets and displaced on the counter. Items from our closets had been wrenched from hangers and left on the floor. Later, my father would hear that one professor from the university had bragged that he'd lain on the carpet in the middle of our living room and listened to our "aura"! It wasn't very good, he said. We gave off a bad vibe.

Our house had become a curiosity, it seemed, simply because we lived in it. Maybe people expected it to hold mysterious Oriental secrets. I for one was glad that we'd safely packed up most of the antiques from my grandparents by this time. Then, while we were in California, my mother at her interview, the bad news came. The loan hadn't gone through. Our house wasn't sold after all.

(Later, in a series of coincidences that seemed quite suspicious, every loan application for our house would fail at the local banks. In fact, no one would ever obtain a loan to buy our house. We would sell it finally, at a loss, nearly a decade later, only because the buyer—a man whom my mother had hired to clean our carpets once and who'd fallen in love with the property—won the Iowa State Lottery and paid cash.)

Then my mother didn't get the job in California. Midway through her campus visit, the university there started receiving phone calls from someone in our town in South Dakota. Crazy calls. Calls asking for my mother, asking if there were any more jobs, asking obnoxious personal questions of whoever happened to be answering the phone. Altogether they received more than a dozen calls in two days, all claiming to be from a "friend" of Carolyn Chai, a concerned friend who wanted to know how her interview was going. Needless to say, the interview did not go very well after that. Thoroughly depressed, we left California and drove the eleven hundred miles back to our farm.

We couldn't figure out what was going on. If people disliked us so much—as they seemed to—they why wouldn't they let us leave? It felt as though we were being punished for crimes we hadn't realized we'd committed: arrogance, urbanity, miscegenation, failure to conform to norms that we hadn't known existed. And that our punishment would be the utter humiliation of my parents, particularly my father. As we would find out later, there were many people who wanted my father to suffer. They were going to do their best to keep him from providing for his family. They were going to show this "Chinaman" his place. We didn't know any of this at the time, however. We learned the truth only when, after years of frustration, my father persuaded a former colleague of his from Redlands who was now a college administrator in Missouri to pose as the head of a search committee and call the university. And then my father learned what his former colleagues in South Dakota were saying about him: Chai's a maverick. He's not a team player. He's a unionist. He's a radical. He's a troublemaker. One man even claimed that my father had communist sympathies. The man laughed when he said it, a nudge-nudge wink-wink kind of joke, meaning that Chai wasn't *really* a communist, but, you know, with his background—City College, labor unions, activists, *all that*—he might as well have been a communist sympathizer.

But in the summer of 1981 we knew nothing of this campaign of humiliation. We only felt the humiliation and could only guess at what was going wrong.

At the end of the summer, my father found a position in Houston as an international educational consultant. He would work with a private foundation that helped foreign students adjust to the American university system. It was a stepping-stone kind of job, with no security, no benefits, no health insurance, and no tenure—not the kind of job he'd been reared since birth to pursue. As the first-born son he was supposed to follow in his father's footsteps, which meant getting a Ph.D. and becoming a professor. His younger brothers were leaving academia to start their own software company, a move that caused my grandfather anxiety. In his day, in China, intellectuals were supposed to teach. There was no higher calling. And every other job was risky. Since Nai-nai's death, Ye-ye had grown thin and frail, and his voice trembled on the phone when we talked. Now my father looked worried every time they spoke.

Ye-ye had always been my father's confidante. While his mother had pushed him to aim for the top, my grandfather was the one who gave him practical advice, how to write a paper, how to choose a topic for a dissertation. They'd written eight books together, father and son, and my father had often called Ye-ye as he prepared his lectures as a professor, to debate certain points of China's political history with him, or simply to get his opinion on an article he was writing.

Although my father's new position as a consultant paid well, far better than his position as vice president had, in fact, he felt ashamed. He was letting his father down. Many nights, I heard him shouting into the phone (Ye-ye was becoming quite deaf), assuring my grandfather that he would do his best to search for another academic post.

Because my father knew he wouldn't stay very long at the consulting job, he and my mother decided it would be better not to uproot the whole family and move to Texas. They decided that my mother, my brother, and I would stay on our farm and my father would commute until he found another teaching position.

Now, every time before he left for Houston, my mother insisted we say a rosary together as a family. We knelt together in the living room, the moonlight flooding around us through the picture window, the statue of Guan Yin in the corner staring serenely over my shoulder. My mother led the prayer, beginning each decade in her soft, steady voice, the rest of us joining in for the second half. In this way we recited the five decades of the rosary—the fifty recitations of the Hail Mary—then finished with the prayer that began "Hail, Holy Mother." I had never learned this prayer, as I'd also decided to quit C.C.D. classes after moving to South Dakota, and so my mother would recite its verses alone.

Sometimes, instead of praying with my eyes closed, I would watch my mother out of the corner of my eye. She had a beautiful profile, a long straight nose, high apple cheekbones, a wide, smooth forehead. As she fingered the beads of her rosary, I wanted to reach out and hold her and be held. I wanted to sit in her lap and listen as she promised me, as she had when I was a child during the turmoil years at City College, that everything would be all right, that we would be fine. But I was no longer a child, and so I merely watched her and my father pray, their lips moving in unison, their own fears so evident on their faces, their eyes squeezed tightly shut, their foreheads creased with lines that had not existed just a few years earlier, their whispering voices barely audible beneath the sound of the wind blowing through the fields outside our house.

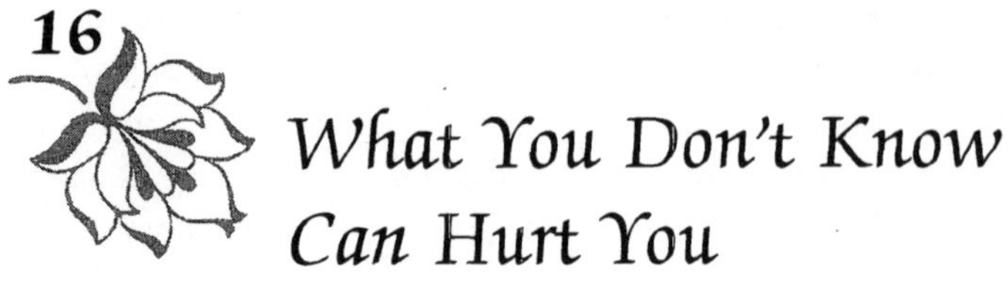

16 What You Don't Know Can Hurt You

Years later, after I'd left home, I used to joke with my brother that if our parents had only seen *Deliverance* instead of *It's a Mad, Mad, Mad, Mad World,* our lives would have been entirely different. Looking back, I could see the signs that said "Don't move to this place!" as clearly as if I were reading yesterday's newspaper. Unfortunately, in 1979, on the cusp of a supposedly bright new decade, my father was as naive as most New Yorkers about the middle of the country, the so-called heartland, the place where small-town values still lived on. But what exactly are small-town values?

In 1979 we knew that the media were critical of the growing trade gap between Japan and the United States. A decade earlier Japan had been known mostly for transistor radios and cheap electronics. By the late 1970s Detroit was reeling from the competition of well-made compact Japanese automobiles, and editorial cartoons lampooned the fact that almost all the electronics Americans were buying were made in Japan. Sony, Honda, Mitsubishi, Toyota were foreign-sounding names in those days, new and thus threatening. But my parents never imagined how the growing rage against Japan's rising economic power, fed by the media looking for a story that would sell papers and boost television ratings, would affect our lives. After all, we were not Japanese.

Similarly, although my parents had read stories about the growing family farm crisis, they'd also read stories like the glowing cover story on agribusiness in *Time* magazine, which made it seem as though only a few farms were in trouble and that most American farmers were modernizing, adapting, thriving even. They were feeding the world, more productive than ever. My father didn't realize that he would be moving his family into a region whose economic base was in fact being devastated. Many small farmers had taken out large loans in the early '70s in order to expand production and buy more acreage, along with the expensive new equipment they needed if they were to remain competitive. But rising interest rates and falling prices for farm products meant that the next decade would see a transformation of the landscape, as banks foreclosed on the loans and farms that had been in a family for five generations were lost: sold to corporations, to strangers. Again, my father didn't see how this related to him. He wasn't trying to hurt the family farmer. As an educator, my father felt that he was on small farmers' side.

Finally, none of us had any idea about the strained race relations between Native Americans and whites in the state.

Four years before we moved to South Dakota, the state put down an uprising on the Pine Ridge Indian Reservation that ended in bloodshed. Two white federal agents died brutally, and an untold number of Indian families were terrorized by the gun battle that took place when federal agents and other law enforcement officials stormed houses on the reservation, looking for Indian activists accused of fomenting trouble. Eventually four Indians who fled the scene were arrested, three tried in Iowa and found not guilty of the agents' murder. The fourth, a man by the name of Leonard Peltier, was tried alone in North Dakota and found guilty, although ballistic records would later show that his gun had not fired the fatal bullet. He was sentenced to life in prison in Leavenworth.

Before the trials of these four men, law enforcement agencies had flooded the Midwest with warnings that Indian radicals would come into the towns where the trials were held and try to disrupt the proceedings. Even the FBI said it feared bloodshed, as the activists would undoubtedly be armed. It was widely reported that these Indian activists wanted to kill white people for revenge. They were assumed to be capable of any kind of atrocity. Under no circumstances should they be trusted.[3]

By this point in 1975, however, the activists in the American Indian Movement had scattered across the country, driven off the reservation by all the violence. In fact, no radicals flooded into small midwestern towns. The trials were not disrupted, nor were there any revenge killings. Still, the memory of these warnings and the rumors that had flooded the countryside did not subside but endured long after the trials were over. The warnings created a fear of Indians probably not seen in the Midwest since the nineteenth century, when the Indians had not yet been driven onto reservations and could still fight for their land.

"The only way to deal with the Indian problem in South Dakota is to put a gun to the AIM leaders' heads and pull the trigger," said William Janklow, a candidate for state attorney general in 1974. He won and later was elected governor, four times.[4]

When we arrived in South Dakota, many people were still reeling from protests and demonstrations by Native American activists. One of the earliest confrontations between activists and police occurred in 1973 at a courthouse in Custer, South Dakota, in the far western part of the state. A riot erupted after someone threw a teargas canister into the building. In the subsequent unrest, two police cars were set on fire and an abandoned building next to the courthouse was burned to the ground. The riot took on a symbolic character, described by one writer as "an historic event, the first outbreak of violence between white men and Lakota since the massacre at Wounded Knee in 1890."[5] Whites were frightened by the violence. Meanwhile, AIM members vowed to help the Lakota tribe regain the Black Hills and the mining rights that had been taken from them, a vow that sent a chill through the state.

[3]Peter Matthiessen, *In the Spirit of Crazy Horse* (New York: Penguin Books, 1992), 282–83.

[4]Ibid., 107. See also Josh Garrett-Davis, "Janklow: Fall of a South Dakota Hero," *Denver Post*, October 20, 2003, 7B.

[5]Matthiessen, *In the Spirit of Crazy Horse*, 63.

Custer was located in the Black Hills, just twenty-two miles southwest of Mt. Rushmore. According to the 1868 treaty that the Lakota signed with the U.S. government, the tribe agreed to give up its right to live on its hunting grounds, which now would be open to white settlers, and would agree to live on a reservation in the Black Hills. At the time, the federal government believed it had found an acceptable solution to the Indian problem, because the Black Hills were not suitable for farming or ranching, the principal economic activities of the white settlers. The Lakota, if not happy, were satisfied at least that they would be able to live in the hills they considered the birthplace of their ancestors, their holy land. After white miners illegally prospecting in the Black Hills discovered gold, the government decided that the land was too valuable to leave in the hands of the Indians and in 1876 forced them to move to the Pine Ridge and Rosebud reservations.[6] An entry in an 1880 issue of the *Congressional Record* described the decision this way: "An idle and thriftless race of savages cannot be permitted to stand guard at the treasure vaults of the nation which hold our gold and silver.... The prospector and miner may enter and by enriching himself enrich the nation and bless the world by results of his toil."[7]

By the 1970s the Pine Ridge Reservation contained the two poorest counties in the nation, with endemic alcoholism, teen suicide, domestic violence, and drug abuse. By this time there was also tribal corruption, leading to the creation of so-called GOON squads, who ostensibly were supposed to enforce tribal law and keep the peace but in fact had turned into a kind of hit squad, extorting money and bribes from the terrorized population. When AIM members arrived in 1973 to try to bring to the reservation the civil rights movement that had been rocking the rest of America, they were treated at first with great suspicion by the Lakota. Gradually AIM convinced many members of the tribe to protest their second-class status in America and to reveal the terror in their lives. This led to the protest at the federal courthouse in the tiny town of Custer.

[6] Ibid., 13.
[7] Quoted ibid., 15.

Naming a town in the Lakota holy land "Custer" is like naming a suburb of Jerusalem "Hitlerville," a slight not lost on the Indians. Furthermore, by taking their protest off the reservation and into the shadow of the famous Mt. Rushmore, they hoped to capture the attention of the national media. They wanted the world to find out about the GOON squads, the violence, the threats, and also what they called the illegal seizure of the Black Hills from the Lakota. It was this last bid that most frightened the government of South Dakota, because in addition to staging protests, the Indians filed a lawsuit in federal court to have the Black Hills returned to the custody of the Lakota Nation under the terms of the treaty of 1868.

Although white ranching and farming were heavily subsidized by the federal government, most of the state's income came from the Black Hills. Gold mines were still in business, and the trademark tri-colored jewelry—yellow, green, and pink from mineral deposits—was much sought after in the world. Tourism to Mt. Rushmore alone accounted for more than 50 percent of the state's revenue. No one in the government wanted to lose the Black Hills.

By 1980, a year after we moved to the state, the U.S. Supreme Court did in fact rule partly in the Lakota tribe's favor, recognizing that their treaty had been illegally and unilaterally broken by the federal government. But rather than award the Indians their land, the Court ruled that they should be adequately compensated. The Lakota refused the settlement and sought new legal grounds on which to file an appeal, insisting that they wanted their land, not compensation money.

This terrified the state government. As he was a new state employee, one of the first things my father was told, during a state legislative session that would decide the university's annual budget, was that everyone would have very tight finances that year because the state needed funds to fight these lawsuits.

When my father raised the question of recruiting new businesses to invest in the state, or luring new industries into the region to offset the lost revenue or even the potential loss of the Black Hills, he was told that he was crazy. One man grew very red in the face and told him outright that South Dakotans didn't want those "mafia-controlled Jewish labor unions" moving in and stirring up trouble. South Dakota was a state of honest people and it was going to stay that way, he insisted.

When my father told us this story, he laughed. He couldn't believe the man was serious. I, on the other hand, couldn't believe he had made us leave New Jersey to live in this place.

Four years after we moved to South Dakota, the National Book Award–winning author Peter Matthiessen published a book about the Indian activists on Pine Ridge called *In the Spirit of Crazy Horse.* He described in detail not only the AIM-led protests but also the GOON squads and the brutal murders of the FBI agents that led to the trials of Leonard Peltier and the three men who were acquitted. He also detailed the deaths of several Indian activists. One of the most incendiary revelations was about our governor, William Janklow, who, Matthiessen reported, had been accused of raping his family's fifteen-year-old Indian babysitter back in 1967, when he was just out of law school and serving as director of the Legal Services Program on the Rosebud Reservation. The girl reported the alleged rape to her principal, who took her to a hospital for an exam. Finding evidence "suggesting an attack had occurred," the physician called the Bureau of Indian Affairs representative so that the girl could file a complaint. Within a week, the girl's mother had been beaten to death and the file on her case had been "lost." Although the governor was never officially investigated for the alleged crime—he left the reservation without waiting for an inquiry—he was subsequently disbarred from practicing law on the reservation ever again by a tribal court judge, Mario Gonzalez, in 1974. Because of the nature of the reservation legal system, the case could not be pursued off the reservation grounds.[8]

The book was a sensation and everyone at the university was gossiping about it, but it was quickly pulled from the shelves of all local bookstores. Shortly after the book was first published in early 1983, the governor filed a lawsuit against Matthiessen, his publisher

[8]Matthiessen, *In the Spirit of Crazy Horse,* 107–9. For the full text of Judge Gonzalez's disbarment opinion, see http://www.dlncoalition.org/dln_issues/janklowdisbarmentopinion.htm.

(Viking) and three South Dakota bookstores that had sold the book, alleging libel and bias.[9]

Various appeals and an additional suit filed by an FBI agent kept the book tied up in court for eight years, and it was finally reissued in paperback in 1991 by Viking Penguin. By then we had left South Dakota, and my mother was able to buy a copy of *In the Spirit of Crazy Horse* in a bookstore in Boulder, Colorado, where I was attending grad school. Only then did we learn about all the terrible, violent things that had occurred just four years before we moved to South Dakota, things that had terrified the white population, creating the atmosphere of distrust, fear, and suspicion that would affect our lives for as long as we lived in Vermillion.

[9] For a full description of the various lawsuits and appeals, see the afterword written by Martin Garbus, in Matthiessen, *In the Spirit of Crazy Horse,* 593–600.

17

Stephen King High

Then came high school.

The violence of the high school was legendary in our town, and starting in eighth grade my brother and some of his friends took up weight lifting in preparation. They felt that a year of concentrated effort might give them the edge they would need to survive freshman year. If a boy went down too easily in ninth grade—no matter the odds, five on one, ten on one—he would hardly make it through the rest of high school. The key was to be able to put up a good fight.

My mother had assured me that I'd like high school more than middle school, as I'd now be able to pick my own classes. "Each year will get better," she said cheerfully. But I remember my disappointment when our very first day of classes, the freshman English teacher wrote on the blackboard a list of grammar rules that he had invented and insisted that we would all follow in our essays or we would not pass. My middle school English teacher—Mrs. Margaret Cash—had been a brilliant teacher, a woman who encouraged us to read diverse books and push our own writing in new directions. She had also been a strict grammarian, with a fondness for diagramming sentences, which had earned her a certain enmity among my classmates. But this new teacher was something I'd never encountered before in school: completely incompetent. For example, he insisted that all "grammatically correct" paragraphs were composed of five to eight sentences, no more and no less. The only exception was the "introductory paragraph," which could contain as few as three sentences but never more than five.

The next day I brought in a book from home, Russell Hoban's *Riddley Walker,* an acclaimed novel set in a postapocalyptic world where humans wander amid the ruins, speaking in a half-remembered, half-invented form of English. I had won the book in a writing contest the year before; otherwise I never would have found it. There was only one tiny bookstore in the town, stocked primarily with romance novels, science fiction, Westerns, and other genre titles that the owner knew would sell.

I showed *Riddley Walker* to my classmates and then to the teacher.

"This book has paragraphs with more than eight sentences and fewer than five," I pointed out.

Our English teacher merely shook his head and told me it didn't count. The other books I brought in didn't count either. The teacher took to interrupting his grammar lessons with longwinded asides about "some people who think they can write" and "some people who only write junk," while staring at me. Sometimes he grew so excited as he spoke that his voice rose louder and louder, his face reddened, and spittle sprayed against the blackboard as he curled his hands into fists and pulled at the bottom of the navy blue windbreaker that he wore to class day in, day out.

He frightened me when he shouted like this, and I decided that all my paragraphs for the rest of the year would contain five to eight sentences, no more, no less.

Every morning, after everyone was inside the school, the vice principal and other male teachers would begin patrolling the hallways, trying to curb the violence between students. Once, when a boy gave a teacher lip, the teacher grabbed the student around the neck and drilled his head into a row of lockers.

After the first bell rang for class, one of these male teachers would have to walk around the exterior of the school, looking for stragglers, for anyone smoking behind the building or spitting their chewing tobacco against the brick walls. Despite this precaution, dried chaw clung to the bricks in clumps like hornet's nests. The patrolling teacher was also responsible for padlocking all the doors from the outside (except for the main entrance, which led to the principal's office and was more heavily patrolled), so that no students could sneak out once classes had begun. As the windows by design only opened a few inches and were reinforced with metal so that the glass could not be broken, I felt as though I were truly locked into a prison. If there were ever a fire inside or a tornado headed our way, we'd all be trapped inside, I pointed out to my classmates, but they only laughed at me, the worrier.

Still, despite these precautions, the boys fought ferociously in the hallways between classes, groups grabbed unsuspecting underclassmen and dashed them to the ground, stomping on their legs or other body parts, grinding faces into metal lockers, into the waxed floor, flesh against flesh, bending and bruising. They snarled like packs of feral dogs. I had seen scenes like this on nature documentaries, but I'd never expected to see such behavior in a school.

I was still so naive, so suburban.

Some days after school, I'd lie on the bed in my parents' room and cry.

"I don't want to go to school anymore," I told my mother once. She was dressing up for some occasion, putting on earrings before the mirror atop the vanity built into the wall.

"Okay," she said. "Don't go." And she meant it; my mother liked to think outside the box.

"But how am I going to learn anything?" I asked immediately. I didn't lift my head from the bedspread, but only watched my mother in the mirror out of the corner of my eye.

"You can teach yourself," my mother replied. "I'll ask the bookstore to see if they can order the textbooks for you."

"I can't teach myself! I won't learn anything!" I began to cry hysterically. My mother joined me on the bed, sitting on the corner, as she stroked my hair anxiously. She patted my back.

"Don't worry. You're very smart. You can be your own teacher," she said confidently, but her face looked worried, her eyebrows drawn together. Deep lines had settled into her forehead, lines that had appeared since we'd moved to this place. I didn't remember them from our life before. They worried me now, the way they made her skin pucker, as though her face were hurting her.

"It's okay," I said at last, when I was sure my voice wouldn't break or warble. "It's only four years."

"And freshman year is the hardest." My mother nodded.

"Next year will be better," I said. "I'm not worried. You shouldn't worry either."

My mother nodded and smiled a little, although the deep lines in her forehead remained.

18

Barbarians

My *father returned from* **Houston** one day to find my brother and me lifting weights in the basement. The metal clanked as we heaved long bars with colored disks on either end above our chests, grunting and sweating. My father stood in the doorway to what had been the ping-pong room before we had turned it into the "weight room," and watched us for quite some time, but we didn't notice him there. Finally, he could stand it no more.

"What are you doing?" he asked.

I was still counting, breathless, unable to answer yet, ". . . five, six, seven . . ."

"What are you doing?" he raised his voice so that we could not ignore him.

My brother turned, his eyes wide and startled. He was my spotter, so I had to struggle to place my weights back on the metal stand above the bench now that he'd been distracted.

"Hey, Pop!" Jeff smiled. "I can bench one-eighty! Wanna see?"

Before our father could respond, Jeff added more weights onto a metal bar and hefted it up to his chest for our father to witness. My brother's face and neck turned a deep scarlet and the veins in his temple throbbed violently beneath his skin.

"Stop it!" our father shouted. "You're crazy!"

Jeff heaved the weight from his chest onto the floor. He looked at our father in a strange, wounded way.

"Hey, Pop," he said after a pause, "even May-lee can bench—"

"You're crazy! You're going to stunt your growth! You're going to ruin your health!" Our father tried to impress upon us the importance of what he was saying by raising his voice. We looked away, embarrassed, humiliated, tired. He tried to think of a way to reach us. "You're becoming . . ." Our father searched for the word he'd heard us say. A word he was sure we would understand. "You're becoming weirdoes! Weirdoes!" he repeated triumphantly. That was indeed the word. He could tell by the way we flinched. "I'm going to tell your mother! Her children are becoming weirdoes!"

I jumped up then and ran past him, up the stairs. I ran to my room and slammed the door loudly, so that I was sure my father would hear, then stomped loudly across the floor as well.

I could picture my brother sitting on his weight bench, flexing his muscles forlornly. He wouldn't look our father in the eye. He would be staring at the floor, at his massive feet in the expensive new sneakers our father had had to buy for him again. Now that he was in high school, my brother was growing rapidly and needed new shoes every few months. He ate endlessly, plate after plate, wolfing his food down without chewing. He was becoming like the boys in this town. Tall, muscular boys. "He's not my son anymore," I'd heard my father say to our mother once. He was no one my father could recognize.

Our father had no idea what our lives were like. He couldn't understand us, the people we were becoming. He expected us to remain children, the kind who rushed to the door the moment he arrived home from his work, eager to hear the funny stories he had prepared to tell us.

We'd received a letter from the school. My mother had tried to hide it from my father, but he found it in one of the kitchen cabinets with the bills and church bulletins she saved every Sunday. Jeff had been fighting on school property. Again. He was always fighting. Naturally, my father yelled at my brother then, at dinner, when he knew we'd be trapped in the kitchen because we were hungry and couldn't bear not to eat.

"You're becoming a barbarian," my father shouted, waving the school's letter in the air. "A barbarian! Just like these peasants! You're no son of mine!" And then with one sweep of his arm, he knocked the bowls of food, our dinner, off the kitchen counter and onto the floor.

After he had yelled like this, my mother started to cry, putting her face into her hands, and then my brother, my huge, enormous brother, taller than I'd ever imagined anyone with our genes could grow, my brother with the muscles, his face tightened and puckered, just as it had when he was a little boy, and he burst into tears. Perhaps my father felt guilty then. Perhaps he wanted to put his arms around Jeff's shoulders, as he had when we were little; perhaps he wanted to tell my brother that everything was going to be okay, Papa was here, Papa was here, but my brother was bigger than my father now and my father was the one who'd made him cry. So my father said nothing but sat quietly back in his chair, swallowing and staring dejectedly at the floor.

I couldn't stand it anymore. I jumped up from my chair and cleaned up the mess on the kitchen floor, ignoring everyone.

I banged the spaghetti pot noisily against the sink. I scraped up all the noodles and the Bolognese sauce, scrubbing the carpet ferociously with a sponge. Then I grabbed up all of our plates and scraped them noisily into the trash and washed them clean, my back to my family. I wanted everyone to feel my fury, rising from my heart like heat. It permeated the entire room.

When I was finished cleaning up, my chin in the air, I pushed past my parents without a word and stomped off down the hall to my room, slamming the door behind me.

Normally I yelled. Normally I shouted back at my father. Anything he said, I'd counter. We could argue like this for hours, until my mother begged us to stop, but nothing my mother said would dissuade me, not tears, not threats. I was stubborn and I had a temper.

Now I ignored my family completely.

From inside my room I could hear my brother jump up from his seat and run outside, the front door banging against the wall. My mother followed him, calling for him to put on a coat. She grabbed one off the coat tree by the door and went running after him. I could hear the wind catch hold of her voice and toss it across the fields.

Looking back, I can almost sympathize with my father.

Sometimes I overheard him talking to my mother in the kitchen. He said he regretted moving here. He should never have come. If he'd only known how his children would turn against him.

And it was true. At dinner, we ignored him. We watched the tiny black-and-white television on the counter. We wolfed down our food, heads close to the plate. He'd been gone all week, another week, and he'd come back to this family that acted like strangers. We didn't ask him how his week had gone. We didn't ask if he was tired from the commute. He had to change planes in Des Moines, then fly to Sioux Falls. His luggage had been lost too many times to count. We'd have to drive back the next day to get it, a 130-mile roundtrip. And then it would be time for him to return to Texas.

We didn't let him tell the funny stories he'd prepared about the idiots he had encountered in his new job at the private educational foundation that helped rich foreign students make the transition into the American university system. What that meant was that he pleaded on their behalf so that they didn't get kicked out for skipping class or flunking rudimentary English-as-a-Second-Language programs. The company arranged tutoring sessions and sometimes hired other, poorer foreign students to help the rich ones study, occasionally even to take notes for them in class. For this he had studied ten years, working on his Ph.D. But he wasn't bitter. Not yet.

Perhaps my father had imagined us laughing together as he discussed his week with his grateful family. He had imagined feeling triumphant as he described how he had mastered another week's worth of trials. A male secretary had lost the checks, everyone's, for the entire month. My father had insisted they write him a new one. He wouldn't leave until they had. He stood his ground in the office, face to face with a bureaucrat who wanted to cut out early on Friday afternoon so he could start drinking well before he drove home. But my father insisted, countering every excuse the program administrator could come up with. "Next week, next week. I don't want you to miss your plane home," the man had the temerity to say, as though he had my father's welfare at heart, as though he thought about my father's happy reunion with my mother, my brother, and me, who would be thrilled to see him again after a week's absence and would rush into his arms the minute he appeared in the door. This was the kind of story he told his colleagues. He certainly didn't tell them how his children ignored him while they lifted weights in the basement. He didn't mention our silent dinners before the blaring TV. In his stories, we were always happy, a loving family, the kind that laughed together. So when the bureaucrats at work told him that he'd have to wait for his paycheck, that it might be a while, another week, as though my father didn't know what was going on, as though he couldn't see right through them, he insisted, "No, today is fine. I'll wait."

And then he sat in a chair directly opposite the bureaucrat's desk, strategically positioned so that it blocked his retreat to the door. My father sat with his legs crossed, his hands folded across his chest, as though he had all the time in the world.

And finally the man had relented, had ordered the male secretary to bring in another check for him to sign, and when my father had it safe in his pocket he raced out of the building and back to his hotel.

Because of that imbroglio, he'd almost missed his plane. He told the taxi driver to step on it, he promised the man a twenty-dollar tip if he could make it to the airport before his plane took off, and the driver had, bless him. Immigrants, they understood the value of twenty dollars. They knew full well that expensive sneakers for their son's enormous feet didn't grow on trees.

But we didn't let my father tell any of his stories. We didn't look at him at all. We stared at the television screen, laughing, until he couldn't stand another minute, until he thought he might explode, all the heat from his guts rising to his head. He could feel the sweat beading on his forehead, pouring down his scalp, nothing there to staunch the flow of water, as he was losing his hair. All the stress. He was fast on his way to becoming a bald man like his own father, his hair thinning no matter how he tried to hide the fact, brushing it over the top of his head, shellacking it in place with the travel-size bottles of hair spray he kept just for this purpose. But he knew what was going on. My father knew. He was growing older. He was being eaten alive, by idiots and meaningless work and all those commuter plane rides.

Now, in his home, in his kitchen, with his own family, before he realized what he was doing, he was shouting. He had the dish of food from the table in his hand and had thrown it to the floor. "There's your dinner! There's your dinner!" he shouted, pointing to the spaghetti at his feet.

We were all staring at him then. My mother, my brother, me.

The idiot people on TV were still guffawing at their own insipid jokes. The canned voices echoed across the kitchen, mocking my father, and he found he had forgotten what he'd so wanted to say to his family now that he finally had our attention.

And then the crying had begun.

When my mother returned to the house, her skin was chilly. Cold air hung around her like a cloak.

Perhaps my father had wanted to put his arms around her. Perhaps he wanted her to turn to him and smile, comfort him, tell him what was happening, reassure him that the children would be all right, that everything would be just fine. God's will be done. By the grace of God, we would all be fine. She used to say such things in the past, whenever little troubles would come up, and it reassured my father, calmed the wild beating of his heart, to see her smile, to hear her calm, confident voice in his ear.

But my mother said nothing now. She took her seat at the kitchen counter, opposite my father, and she put her head back in her hands. She wasn't crying anymore. She simply sat like this, unmoving, as I observed from the hallway, crouching in the shadows.

Perhaps my father wanted to reach out and touch her thin shoulders, her long wrists, her graceful fingers, but he found his arms had grown heavy. They hung at his sides, useless. Instead, he watched her sitting like this for some time.

"I'm sorry," he said at last, and that's when my mother began to sob earnestly, her shoulders heaving, with a terrible sound, like a person drowning on dry land.

19 Glamour Puss

Everyone has a moral line in the sand that cannot be crossed. For my parents it was hearth and home. They weren't going to give up their house. Both of them had led nomadic childhoods, for different reasons but with the same result: they weren't going to lose their South Dakota farm without a fight. One afternoon my mother and I were shopping in the Piggly Wiggly, when a cart rounded the corner and the wife of one of the other vice presidents came into view. She looked startled to see us, and for a second her face flushed, her eyes darted to the side, as though she were looking for an easy way to back up and head in the opposite direction. But then the panic settled, hardened. And she pushed her cart, looking straight ahead as though we were invisible, as though we weren't standing right there in front of the peanut butter and jam jars.

"Hello, Mrs. St—" my mother called out, her voice strong.

The woman stopped behind her cart and eyed my mother icily. "Oh, you're still here? Not homeless yet?"

"Homeless!" The woman must have imagined that she was being clever, but now my mother was furious. Her Irish was up, as she used to say. My mother smiled so that all her teeth showed. She was going to bite this woman in two. "Ha! What a joker you are. We've never been better! Winberg is very happy traveling with his consultancy job. In fact, we're expanding the farm. Chickens, cows, goats. It's so wonderful, this wholesome life. What a funny, funny person you've become!"

The vice president's wife didn't know what to say. Her lips twitched. She wanted to smile or sneer but her mouth wouldn't obey and gaped open instead.

My mother flashed her smile—her teeth were blinding—and I followed her quickly down another aisle.

By now, in 1982, we knew what was being said behind my father's back. We knew why he wasn't getting any of the academic jobs he was applying for.

Can we sue them? My mother wanted to know.

Not without a lot of money, my father thought. Besides, he added, the publicity could be just as damaging. People would think there had to be some truth, something terrible to justify the animosity. Administrators were suspicious by nature. They wanted to avoid controversy.

"There's no hope," my father said. "They want to destroy me. They want to destroy my career."

He decided to continue his consulting work, and in the meantime he'd try to wait the situation out. The young president who'd first hired my father had already left the university, left academia altogether to go into business, but the vice presidents were still around. They were applying for other jobs, trying to move up the chain of command. Once they left, maybe he'd have a chance.

"We just have to hold on for a while," he told my mother.

Sometimes my father returned from Texas in a good mood. For Christmas he brought us unusual gifts, exquisite things we'd never seen before and couldn't find in our town. For my mother he bought long leather gloves with mink cuffs, a jade necklace with a pendant carved into a monkey clutching a peach. "Where am I going to wear something like this?" my mother exclaimed, laughing. She slipped the necklace over her neck, then tried the gloves on, holding her long fingers up before her eyes.

"Wear them anywhere. Everywhere. To the grocery store!" my father laughed too. He took her right hand in his and kissed the back of her gloved wrist.

For my brother there were exotic toolkits, miniature pens that unscrewed and turned into screwdrivers, Swiss Army knives that unfolded with kitchen utensils and lock-picking devices, multiblade knives and scissors that could cut through sheet metal. For me there was a jade-colored sweater from the Gap—a store I'd seen advertisements for in magazines but had never been inside—and a pair of Texas-weight legwarmers, red and white striped. The legwarmers fascinated me. They were silky and soft but completely worthless in terms of warmth. When I pressed them to my cheek, I thought I could smell the heat of Houston. I kept them in the pockets of my down coat. When I reached inside, instead of the mounds of snow around us, the howling wind, the steel-sharp air, I would rub my fingertips against the silky legwarmers and feel the bright sunlight of Texas glittering off the skyscrapers, the highways, the glass and steel of the city. In the middle of another long Dakota winter, I longed for nothing so much as warmth.

But sometimes, when my father returned home, he fell into a depression. Nothing we did could please him then. He sat at the kitchen counter, muttering to himself. He complained to us whenever either my brother or I came into the room, looking for something to eat. We were going to ruin him! he shouted. We spent too much money, we ate too much food, we always needed this or that. We were weights chained to his ankles, rocks piled on his chest, knives in his back. If he'd only known when he was a young man how his family would turn out, he said, he never would have gotten married.

Years passed like this.

By the time I was fifteen and a half, I had given up trying to fit in here. I was merely trying to survive. The stares people gave me were changing. Now grown men sidled up to me on the sidewalk, came up to me after church gatherings, at community picnics, at wedding receptions. They wanted to tell me about the hookers they'd known in Vietnam, on R&R in Thailand, in the Philippines, in Taiwan.

"They had the best girls on Taiwan. They used to send them over on the backs of mopeds," a former fighter pilot named Bob told me once.

"Oh, really?" I said, because I had been taught to be polite to my elders and I had no words in those days to describe how creepy Bob made me feel. I didn't know how to refuse his attention. We were in a public place, on a sunny day, many people around us. It was a potluck of some sort, but everyone at the picnic tables seemed so far away, their voices retreating. The wind was rushing through the trees, and that was the sound that was suddenly in my ears, the whoosh of leaves trembling.

"They put us up in this really fancy place, I can still remember the name, the Tai-bao, they called it. Do you know what that means? I think they said it meant palace. I remember that word. Can't forget it. Tai-bao."

Bob was growing misty-eyed. He wasn't even looking at me anymore but off at the sky, into the middle distance. I was watching him from the corner of my eye while pretending to stare at my sneakers. It was as though he'd left me and wandered off into his memories. I should have turned and run, but I couldn't move.

"They used to put these little fortune cookies in the nightstand drawer. The top one. I remember one night I opened my fortune and it said, 'You will live to see your many descendants like gold in your pocket.' Man, 'like gold in your pocket.' That was the most beautiful thing anyone could have told me. I carried that piece of paper with me everywhere, every mission, every run. We'd drop our load and watch the explosions open up like flowers, like liquid gold, and I'd think about that little piece of paper." Bob was getting emotional, wiping his eyes on the back of his fist, and then he was digging into his back pocket, pulling out the wallet attached by a chain to his belt. "Yep, yep, I still have it with me." And sure enough, he pulled out a tiny slip of paper from between the dollar bills, and he read it aloud to me again, underlining each word with his forefinger as he went along. I was so fascinated by this performance that for a moment I forgot this was happening to me. I actually felt sorry for Bob. He was really old, and not just in the way that all adults are old to a sixteen-year-old. He was thinning-hair-and-grizzly old. He was bad-skin old. Too-much-drink, too-many-drugs old. His rambling voice, talking to himself about his memories, was old, and I was suddenly aware of my youth and how I would never ever be this sentimental about a fortune cookie. Bob's life was behind him.

I wanted to ask Bob if it was true, if he had lived to see his many descendants, but his mind had wandered off somewhere else. Then, just as suddenly, Bob snapped back to the present. He blinked his eyes and smiled blankly at the picnic tables laden with church potluck, with taco salads and molded Jell-O parfaits with fruit and Cool Whip in alternating layers, the tater tot casseroles and tuna casseroles and Hamburger Helper casseroles, and the punch cups filled with Kool-Aid arranged in columns on top of the red gingham checked plastic tablecloths. Bob had lost his train of thought, he had forgotten about me, and he wandered off, shaking his head, disappearing into a noisy crowd of teenagers playing Frisbee.

Because of men like Bob, I took to wearing baggier and baggier clothing, slouching so that I'd appear shorter and younger. I persuaded my mother to give my straight, dark hair perm after perm, using the Toni Super-Hard-to-Curl home kits, leaving the chemicals on for an hour past the recommended time. My hair turned orangish and frizzy, and from behind no one could tell I was Asian. I felt pleased, not because I thought looking more Caucasian was superior to looking Asian—I didn't—but because I imagined that I was blending in with my surroundings. I convinced myself that my pouffy hair made me look like my classmates, like the people in our town. I was camouflaged. But from the front, I couldn't hide: my round face gave me away. My disguise fooled none of these men, and they continued to seek me out to tell me stories about the war.

There was a retarded girl at school whom many of my classmates liked to throw food at during lunch. I had taken to walking with her every day so that I could yell at the kids who attacked her; only then would they stop. As a result of my behavior, my old friends no longer spoke to me. They couldn't understand why I wanted to hang around with a retarded girl. Sometimes they tried to throw food at her, too. All of my former friends were in the honors program like me. They were considered the smart girls. Strivers. We'd never been really close, but we ate together in the cafeteria at lunch, mainly because we fit into no other group; the popular girls had boyfriends to eat with; the hoodlum girls ate together in tight packs, ready for a fight. I remembered these girls from junior high. Some of them had been considered smart girls, too, but once they started dating, they made sure their grades dropped to acceptable C's. Only losers without boyfriends still needed to get A's.

Boys in our school didn't need to study, either, unless they were "faggots." It was widely understood that fags studied because they weren't going to inherit land from their fathers; they were losers, just like us girls who studied and who weren't going to inherit farms, either. The other boys beat up the faggots in the hallways and after school. Everyone understood this, even the teachers, who conveniently looked the other way when the faggots got their heads smashed against lockers or flushed in the girls' room toilets or simply body-slammed between classes.

There was only one girl in my loser, striver group whom I truly admired. Her name was Lola. She was very smart, studied all the time, and was a star basketball player. I liked to compete with her in our honors science classes. She was also extremely beautiful. She was half white and half Lakota, but her features tended toward the Indian in her. She had skin the color of a light charcoal wash, jet-black shiny hair, and hazel eyes. Girls like Lola had stared down from billboards in New York City, urging us to buy cars or makeup or Florida orange juice. They advertised new shades of lipstick with names like Mystique and Glamour Puss and Exotique. But here, behind Lola's back, the white boys made fun of her.

"Why is her hair so greasy all the time? Doesn't she ever take a shower?"

"Why is her skin so dark like that? It makes her look dirty."

It was expected that girls, popular and unpopular, should laugh when boys made jokes, but I told them off instead. I was so far away from being popular, it didn't matter to me anymore what names my classmates called me. I thought I had grown immune to their insults.

The retarded girl whom I befriended tended to talk in a monologue, neither expecting nor waiting for a reply. She chattered about her dog and her grandmother, a boy she liked, the new Walkman her grandmother had purchased for her. She told the same stories over and over. If I asked her questions, she grew confused and frustrated, so I stopped asking questions, and she spoke in her soliloquies as we walked together through the halls of the high school, round and round, round and round. Sometimes I conjugated French verbs in my head. I'd just been granted permission to attend a French class at the university that fall, three times a week, after petitioning for years. *Je vais, tu vas, il va, nous allons, vous allez, ils vont.* We passed my classmates in the hallways as we walked in circles. Their faces loomed close, then disappeared. I focused on only pieces of their bodies, for we walked too fast to see them clearly. There were laughing mouths, chewing mouths, open and closed mouths, whispering mouths, grinning lips, thin lips, little sharp teeth, large horse teeth, yellow teeth that needed to be brushed. *Je fais tu fais il fait, nous faisonsvousfaitesilsfont.*

One day Lola interrupted our walk. I was surprised to see her. She'd stopped talking to me along with the other girls in my erstwhile lunch group, but now she smiled at me.

"Come on, May-lee, what are you doing?" She gestured for me to follow her around a corner. The retarded girl followed us both.

"No," Lola commanded, nodding at the retarded girl. "Leave her!"

"She's a really nice person," I heard my voice speaking. "You'd like her." Although it wasn't true, I knew. I was lying. Lola wouldn't like the retarded girl.

"Just leave her!" Lola was furious. She gritted her teeth.

The retarded girl reached out for my hand. She was afraid. "It's okay," I lied. "Everything's okay."

Lola scowled, shook her head, and disappeared down the hall.

I knew then that I had been wrong. I wasn't as strong as I thought. I could still be hurt.

Years later, long after I had left home, long after I'd left this town and graduated from college and was working as a reporter in Denver, my mother called me one day to tell me about the death of a kid I used to know, a boy on my bus route. She'd just heard the news from a friend. The boy had committed suicide. He was seventeen or eighteen years old.

He'd been a member of the football team, maybe even the quarterback, and for homecoming the team had apparently gang-raped a retarded girl at a party outside town limits. The story didn't come out for a while, not until the season was over and wrestling in full swing, when the whispers and the rumors became impossible to ignore and one of the coaches even promised an investigation. Then the boy had killed himself.

Everyone was shocked. *Such a tragedy. His whole life had been ahead of him.* The investigation had stopped then. There seemed no point in going on. *Why add salt to a wound?* I knew how people in our town used to talk. I could imagine what they were saying now.

My mother and I both knew this boy. Or rather had known him when he was a child. When I was twelve and he was eight, we'd ridden on the same bus to school. He'd been a funny kid, always telling jokes, very cheerful. Our bus driver was an alcoholic and he often drove off the gravel and into the ditches that lined the country roads. This kid used to give the bus driver a hard time about it, making us all laugh. He wasn't afraid of the bus driver's threats. Once he'd plucked a dandelion from the middle of his lawn and eaten the head off on a dare. He was just a silly, funny little kid.

Another time, one of his father's cows had gotten loose from their pasture and ended up in our brome field, several miles from their farm. The boy had come looking for the cow, and when he found it, nothing he did would make it go home with him. He tried roping it around the neck and then pulling and pushing it, prodding it every which way, but it refused to budge. Finally my mother had lured it out of our field and into the back of his truck with a bucket full of corn. The boy had been so grateful. He'd thanked my mother a hundred times.

Of course, by the time he was in high school, he'd started to drink heavily, like most of the kids in town. There wasn't much else to do.

My mother speculated that he hadn't actually been involved in the rape. Just his teammates, not him. He wasn't that kind of boy.

The afternoon he'd killed himself, he'd come home from school the same as any day. His mother was in the kitchen, dinner was in the oven, and she'd wanted to know if he wanted apple brown betty for dessert or Cool Whip Jell-O parfaits. He said, "Jell-O, Mom," which wasn't a surprise because he was not a fancy kind of boy. He liked meat and potatoes and Jell-O all right, no complaints, and he went upstairs to his room. Then she heard the gunshot. By the time she reached his bedroom, he was already dead. There wasn't so much as a note.

The boy's mother had told all the details to anyone at the memorial service who would listen.

My mother speculated that the boy hadn't been depressed about the rape at all, since he couldn't have been involved, but rather over other things. His father's drinking and the DUI he'd garnered that week. The local paper printed the list of DUIs every Tuesday. The boy had been humiliated for his father and then he'd done something rash. I thought the boy was used to his father's DUIs, but I didn't say this to my mother. I let her do all the talking.

My mother was saddened by the news. "It's just such a shock," she said over and over. "Such a nice boy." I suppose I should have been sad, too, but I remember thinking that at last this boy had found a way to escape our town. He wasn't the kind of boy who would go to college or even join the military. He'd never been a particularly good student, as there was no point. Everyone knew he was going to inherit the family farm, which meant that he couldn't leave, so he'd been a happy-go-lucky student, cheerful, friendly, the kind of kid who went with the flow.

Now he wouldn't have to live with his guilty conscience. He wouldn't become a drunk like his father. Instead, he'd surprised everyone and left town.

I didn't worry about this boy anymore. He had found peace. I couldn't hate him, either. He was the only one of those boys who'd shown any kind of remorse.

Instead I worried that the retarded girl might have been the girl I'd known. Perhaps she'd learned to trust too easily because of me. She used to duck her head anytime anyone approached; she'd hunch her shoulders and walk as fast as she could to the girls' room to hide. But after I started walking with her, she'd begun to relax. She smiled at people. She stopped ducking her head. Maybe she'd let her guard down when the boys had put on sweet voices, and instead of running from them maybe she'd gotten in their car, gone to their party, followed them down the rickety stairs to the basement of the abandoned farmhouse, and was raped repeatedly by them and the broomstick and the emergency storm candles and the blunt metal objects they had found and put to this use.

I asked my mother to see if she could find out who the girl was, but none of her friends knew anything about her except that she was retarded.

Was it a sign of the pain our town was going through? So much fear as the economy spiraled away and farms were lost or threatened, five generations of toil come to naught?

Was it the harshness of the weather? The long, terrible winters when the temperatures dropped to seventy below zero with the wind-chill factor, the snow drifts taller than cars, the blizzard winds that howled like a woman shrieking—literally, the first time I heard such a wind, I thought someone was trapped outside, dying—was it the winter?

Was it caused by living in the shadow of genocide, all the deaths that had had to occur before the land could be cleared for farms and ranches and our town? Was it the murders, the cavalry attacks, the reprisals, the battles between the native tribes and the European settlers, wave after wave of violence for generations that hardened people?

Was it the alcohol abuse? Inbreeding? Boredom?

Was it a curse?

20

The Cannibals

When I was sixteen, my father left the Texas job and took a new position in Chicago, working as a consultant for a historically African American educational foundation. He helped them raise funds, recruit members, organize conferences and workshops, network and expand. The new job didn't pay as well as the old one, but he'd grown weary of Texas. Sometimes working in Chicago made him a happier person, and sometimes it only reminded him of all the reasons he hated our town in South Dakota. When he came home, he yelled constantly at my brother and me, but mostly at my brother, because he was growing up and becoming someone my father didn't recognize anymore. My father was anxious all the time.

My mother opened a business in town, a photography studio. She thought it would help us to belong. She would make her own connections to the community, she would find a way for us to survive. I worked in her studio after school and on weekends. I worked on our farm in the mornings before school, before I went to work in the studio, forty hours a week, sixty during school vacations. I didn't realize then that my mother thought if I worked in the family businesses, she could keep me safe from local predators. All I knew was that she, too, was anxious all the time.

On our farm, the chickens were aging. They were no longer laying regularly, the roosters fought savagely, and we couldn't afford to keep feeding them. Early one morning my brother and I rounded them up from their pen and put them in the bed of his pickup truck, which we covered with a green tarpaulin so they couldn't escape. He drove them to the chicken-processing plant—the abattoir—in South Sioux City, Nebraska, and the next day my mother and I picked up their plucked and plastic-wrapped bodies. We now had meat to last through the winter. Unfortunately, I'd made the mistake of naming the chickens after my favorite writers. It had seemed amusing when they were alive, but now I could recognize them in our freezer. The plump one was Ray Bradbury, the one with the skinny thighs, Isaac Asimov. Louisa May Alcott had the uneven, lumpy back, and Emily Dickinson, oh dear, I'd recognize that neck anywhere. There was nothing else to eat, but after Ray Bradbury came out of the broiler, well browned and basted in his own juices, I couldn't bear to eat him. He tasted like sand in my mouth.

My brother said I was a wimp, that I'd never be a real farmer.

That year my brother was intent upon becoming just that. He was going to make the farm practical. He was going to contribute, he said, to help our finances. Since there were still no prospects of selling the house, we all knew by this point that we needed all the help we could get.

We'd built up a regular customer base for our hens' eggs over the past couple of years, but now my brother decided a few dozen layers were too impractical for real farming. He decided to order a scientifically bred super-chicken that was guaranteed to lay an egg every twenty-four hours. I remember the picture in the chicken catalog of a rather scrawny white bird with oddly long legs. It was a new kind of American White Leghorn, "definitely not your grandfather's chicken," the description read, and the bird had a Dewey decimal number after its name to prove it. Because my brother wanted to go into egg production big time, he ordered an initial shipment of seventy-five chicks.

The chicks were cute and harmless looking, all yellow fuzz and soft peeps, and remarkably uniform. They didn't vary in size much, they grew at the same rate, they pooped at the same rate. Maybe we'd simply gotten better at raising chicks, but it seemed as though they didn't have any of the frailties our old chickens had had. They didn't eat the wood chips on the floor and get their anuses plugged with splinters and die of constipation. They didn't catch cold and die of pneumonia if they fell asleep too far from the heat lamps. They didn't dehydrate and desiccate if they slept directly under them, either. Indeed, they seemed like the ideal chicken. My brother and his friends wanted to name them all after Arnold Schwarzenegger, despite the gender issue, because of their remarkable strength. As for me, I thought of them as the THX-1138 birds. Later, we would come to refer to them simply as the Cannibals, but in the beginning we were quite enthusiastic.

The first hint of the problems to come developed when the birds hit adolescence. This is an ugly time for chickens as for humans, a time of molting and the odd feather sticking awkwardly from a downy neck, unwieldy wings, the sudden appearance of lobes of red flesh on the top of the head. The chicks stopped peeping and started clucking loudly. They hopped about in an ungainly fashion, shitting prodigiously. They also began to lay eggs.

Pullet eggs are quite small, only an inch or two in length. They are often rather thin-shelled. They'll crush in your hand if you're not careful. We soon discovered that the scientifically bred White Leghorns enjoyed eating each other's eggs. All chickens will do this, given the opportunity. It's some kind of natural quest for protein. But, if allowed to continue, it can seriously cut into your profit margin. As with our previous layers, my brother had wanted to let the chickens have free run of their coop. He figured that a happy hen would be more likely to lay regularly than an unhappy, pent-up one. To keep the chickens from getting into the habit of eating the eggs, he built a series of wooden roosts for the birds, a series of laying boxes on one wall and a stacked series of perches on the other. Thus the birds would have places to "hide" their eggs, which was normal behavior for a hen that had just laid an egg, and then, when they forgot about the egg, usually after a few minutes, the eggs would still be out of sight of the others so that we could gather them easily. Out of sight, out of mind, Jeff reasoned.

It was a good plan, except that these super-hens seemed to have nothing on their minds but the quest for eggs to eat. They ran about the coop helter-skelter, nervous and high strung, pecking on the floor, pecking in the laying boxes, pecking at the straw, searching for eggs. If they found one, there was a feeding frenzy as all the neighboring hens pressed close, squawking and flapping their wings, trying to get a bite.

And then the pullets grew into adult chickens.

My brother and I were in the barn one evening, filling buckets with corn to bring to the cows in their pole shed behind the barn, when we heard an exceptionally loud series of squawks. They sounded like shrieks from hell, actually.

"Rats!" my brother exclaimed, and he grabbed a hammer off the wall. He wasn't going to lose any more of his chickens to rodents, which we had discovered liked nothing more than to suck the blood out of a sleeping bird. When we'd first started raising chickens, we couldn't figure out what was going on. In the morning we'd find the collapsed bird on the floor of the coop. A wild dog or coyote or fox would have dragged it off to eat, but there was the limp body for all to see, the other chickens still snoozing peacefully nearby. It was only after my brother inspected a body carefully, found the bite marks, and noticed the lack of blood that he realized what was happening. After that, he'd set about making the coop rat-proof. The floor was concrete, which kept rats from burrowing underground, but now he also sealed off the small door in the side of the wall, which we had previously left open so that the birds could leave the coop and walk into their outdoor pen. Then he'd rat-proofed their outside pen, digging a foundation and lining it with chicken wire that ran up the sides of the metal fence, before spreading the dirt and straw back on top. After all that work, no rat should have been able to get into our coop. Yet we could plainly hear a chicken clucking shrilly as though it were being attacked. What kind of über-rat were we dealing with? we wondered.

As we burst into the coop, we smelled the blood before we actually saw the injured hen. But the culprit was no rat. What we discovered was that all the hen's sisters were gathered around, pecking at her body with their tiny, sharp beaks, swallowing her blood in gulps, ripping her flesh from her still living body, even as she shrieked. It was like a scene out of an all-chicken version of *Night of the Living Dead.*

My brother immediately moved into the fray, kicking the chickens apart with his boots. They resisted, flinging themselves at his legs, beating their wings against his jeans, attacking him with their beaks.

"Wait, I'll get the gloves!" I shouted, but my brother knew there was no waiting. He reached into the throbbing mass of chickens with his bare hand and pulled out the body of the dying hen. He snapped her neck to end her suffering and quickly carried her out of the coop and into the barn.

I put on the pair of yellow rubber kitchen gloves that I kept for disgusting tasks and then held open a black Hefty trash bag for him to drop the dead chicken into. While I double-bagged, then triple-bagged the dead bird, Jeff went back into the coop with a broom and swept up all the bloody straw. He cleaned the floor and washed the splashes of blood off the other hens, off their feet and feathers, so that the smell of blood wouldn't make them continue to attack each other.

In truth, almost all chickens have this instinct. Something about the smell of blood drives them into a vampiric state. This is why it was so important to keep the chickens' yard and coop clean, no broken things, no pieces of wire, no sharp edges. Hens will peck their own chicks to death if any of them starts to bleed from an injury. God only knows why. It hardly seems like a healthy evolutionary trait. Perhaps chickens know they are weak, prone to infection, and need to kill off the sick and injured before they infect the flock. I have no idea.

But our new super-chickens were particularly vicious. As they reached adulthood, they began to attack each other with greater frequency, trying to actually draw blood and kill each other rather than wait for an accident. They had excellent fighting instincts, they were good at feints and dodges, and they were fast, so it wasn't all that easy for them to kill each other until they learned to gang up on one hapless hen at a time.

Now we had a crisis on our hands.

My brother had spent a lot of money on these hens and he'd hoped we'd make a profit when they began to lay regularly. It was money that we really couldn't afford to lose. He talked it over with my mother and decided to order some cages from a supplier in Minnesota and had them sent special delivery. Of course, this solution cost even more money, but he figured it was the only way to save the flock and not lose his entire investment.

One of my brother's friends came over to help us assemble the metal cages the night after they arrived. It was a school night and it took us until well past ten to finish putting them together. By midnight we had the birds in their cages, row after row, in three layers. The floors slanted toward a metal channel that ran the length of each row. This channel would catch the eggs as soon as they were laid and keep them safe so that the hens couldn't eat them. There was a long metal trough that ran in front of the cages where we could put their food, and a plastic trough for water.

The hens didn't like being caged. They glared at us in anger, straining their necks between the wires as though they thought they might be able to squeeze out entirely.

We'd only had time to construct one set of cages, which was shaped like the letter "A," with three tiers of about ten cages per row on both sides of the stand. It was late, it was a school night, and we were tired. My brother's friend had to go home. Because there were not enough cages to hold each chicken individually, we tried doubling them up.

But now, as we prepared to leave, we discovered the hens were fighting with their roommates. Savagely. They were pecking at each other, and because they had no room to maneuver, several were able to draw blood rather quickly. Smelling the blood, all the chickens began to call out, squawking and shrieking and straining against their cages, trying to reach the wounded bird, their beaks opening, their tongues extended. They all wanted a bite.

"Damn chickens!" Jeff began jerking open the cages—they had a little trap door on top whose bars could be squeezed together so that it opened—and pulling out birds, one from each cage and tossing them back into the coop.

I put on my yellow rubber gloves with dread. I grabbed a trash bag.

"You get the rest of the chickens!" my brother said. "I'm gonna start building the rest of the cages." He then hurried into the coop and began hammering away. This last set of cages would have to be affixed to the wall, as the coop was too small for the stand.

I managed to pull the live hens from the cages rather easily. By this time in my life on the farm, I had no trouble picking up chickens. I knew how to press the wings to the body and hold the bird tightly under my arm until I deposited it on the floor. With her wings pinned, a chicken never struggled, never even pecked. But now I discovered that two chickens had died; they'd bled to death that quickly. I took the live birds out of the cages around them. They were frenzied but they calmed down once I'd pinned their wings. Pulling the dead birds out was something else. Upon dying, the hens had clenched their talons firmly along the wire bottom of the cage. As I tried to pull one body from its cage, I met with resistance, as the feet would not unhook from the wire. I tried to yank the body but soon realized that this action might rip it in half.

"Fuck!" I shouted at the chickens. "Mary, help me! Fuck! God in Heaven! Fuck, fuck, fuck!"

Leaning over the bottom row of cages while the birds craned their necks through the wires and pecked at my clothes, I reached to the bottom of the cage and tried to unwrap the chicken's talons from their death grip on the wire. Although I was wearing gloves, I could feel the bumps on the skin of the chicken's feet. I could feel the sharp, smooth nails. After I had succeeded in unwrapping one foot from its perch, the toes snapped back into their curled position around my index finger.

I began screaming as loudly as I could.

My brother was hammering and didn't hear me.

I was a wimp, a wimp, a wimp. I was not a farmer, I was not a farmer, I was not a farmer.

I pulled my finger loose and the rubber glove tore.

"Fuckin' A! Fuckin' A! Fuckin' A!" I shouted.

"B-b-b-rrrr-uuuckkk!" some sixty chickens replied.

I gritted my teeth, reached into the cage, and began to break the dead chicken's toes, one by one, to loosen their grip on the wire. Finally the bird came shooting out of the cage, out of my hand, arcing through the air, before landing with a terrible splat on the concrete floor.

Swearing as loudly and vilely as humanly possible for a sixteen-year-old virgin, I picked up the chicken's body and stuffed it into a doubled Hefty bag. I knotted the ends and threw the bag into a corner for Jeff to remove later. Then I went back to get the next dead chicken.

By the time we had finished penning the rest of the hens, cleaning the blood from the floor of the barn and the coop, and spreading fresh, clean straw on the concrete floor, it was nearly three in the morning.

We trudged back to the house in silence, too exhausted to speak.

The blue-white light from the mercury-vapor lamp made our shadows spill from our bodies into two long, thin lines, like a pair of chopsticks splintering.

I felt like crying. All that work, and in two hours it would be time to rise again, if we were to finish all our morning farm chores before school. I wanted to collapse on the frost-covered grass, to fall down and never get up. But gradually a numbness began to spread through my body, originating in my heart and traveling through my arteries to my limbs, to my feet and hands, to my aching shoulders and throbbing head. Finally, all my fatigue settled into a ball in the very pit of my stomach.

I was becoming a farmer, all right.

Every day now I rose before dawn to complete my chicken-related chores. By winter, these chores gave me quite a workout. We could no longer hook a hose to the outdoor water pump; instead, I had to pump individual buckets of water and carry them, two at a time, into the barn to fill all the watering troughs. Then I had to carry bucket after bucket to refill the cows' giant metal water tank. I was growing stronger than I'd ever been in my life. I had ripped muscles on my triceps. I had to carry forty-, sixty-, and seventy-five pound bags of grain from the garage to the barn, and I had to be able to lift a 150-pound bale of alfalfa from one end of the loft to the window where I could throw it to the cows below. I lifted weights, practiced jumping jacks and sit-ups, ran in place in the basement, and skipped rope. My heart rate slowed to forty-four beats per minute.

I wasn't just a kid from the suburbs anymore. I was a country kid, I realized with a kind of astonished pride, although when I found a dead chicken, as I did occasionally—when one of the wild mixed breeds that had escaped from our coop years ago froze in the snow of the goat fort while trying to seek shelter from a storm, or when one of the caged birds got dehydrated because the water trough developed a bend (if the ice formed in just the right spot, the chickens at the far end of the cages didn't get any water)—I still had to put on my rubber gloves to pull out the body, and my stomach still lurched as I carefully broke the toes free, one by one by one.

Once, as I was watering the chickens in the barn, I felt something odd and itchy on my back. I put the bucket down, pulled off my gloves, and tried to scratch between my shoulder blades when all of a sudden I felt the distinct sensation of something running up my back. It was a mouse trapped in my snowsuit! Screaming, I unzipped the suit and, kicking off my boots, ripped the suit from my body, and, still screaming, spun the suit around and around my head with one hand, until I felt a shift in the weight and heard a *thwack* as the mouse launched free and hit the back wall. Still in a panic, I stripped off my overalls, my long-sleeved shirt, my T-shirt, and stood in the middle of the barn in my bra and underpants, patting frantically at my body. I couldn't rid myself of the sensation of little paws running up and down my skin. Finally, I couldn't stand it any longer, and just bent over and started shrieking over and over, as loudly as I could.

The chickens apparently found my behavior curious. They were all looking at me, their tiny shining eyes unblinking in their cages. When I was finished, a few began to buck, and then they began to stick their necks through the cage wires and peck at their empty feed troughs rather savagely, like prisoners running tin cups against the bars of their cells.

I calmed down, put my clothes back on—patting each item carefully with my hands to make sure no more mice had gotten wrapped up in the cloth—and finished feeding the chickens.

On weekends, I had to shovel the chicken shit. The main barn was not too bad, because the cages were staggered and the shit landed on the barn floor and could be scraped up with a shovel and dumped into plastic trash bags, which my brother than took to a back field far from the barn and emptied. But the chickens in the coop were in three parallel rows of cages. My brother had put metal plates between the layers to catch their droppings so that the top two layers wouldn't be pooping on the chickens below, but unfortunately the accumulation of shit was so heavy that the metal plates didn't just slide out easily to be cleaned, as my brother had hoped. Instead, I had to take a large snow shovel and physically scoop the feces from each layer. It was a laborious process that took about four hours to complete. Four hours stuck in the close, smelly coop. What's worse, I discovered that the chicken droppings were infested with millions of squirming white maggots.

Because this was obviously the most disgusting job on earth, I had to think of ways to keep myself from getting utterly depressed doing it. I carried a list of irregular French verbs in my pocket, which I would remove, study quickly, and then recite at the top of my lungs at the chickens, over and over, "Que je vins, que tu vins, qu'il vint . . ." I would memorize one conjugation and move on to the next. My written French improved dramatically, if not my conversational skills.

By midwinter we were indeed a working farm, selling enough dozens of eggs per week to pay for the chickens' feed. Altogether we were pulling in sixty to seventy eggs per day. The chicken catalog had been right about one thing—these super-chickens really did lay well. In fact, after we accidentally left the light in the barn on all night, we discovered that some of the hens could be coaxed to lay twice a day. Every night I had to wash the shit off the eggs, throw away the cracked ones, and set them to dry in the wire egg baskets we kept in the kitchen before putting them into cartons for sale. We had a number of regular customers, including a health-food grocery store, a college sorority, and a couple of restaurants.

Still, we often had many eggs left over. Jeff and I ate as many as we could, fixing omelettes and soufflés and, once, when we were snowed in for the weekend and couldn't make our egg deliveries, an unleavened pancake-like bread that my brother invented using a cup or two of flour and ten eggs. Even when we were thoroughly sick of eggs, we knew that if we didn't eat them they'd start to pile up, and there was no more room in the refrigerator. We began feeding them to the dogs, and their coats grew remarkably thick and shiny. They looked like dogs whose fur was shampooed and blow-dried every morning in a fancy salon. Pouffy dogs.

Working as we did, my brother and I were hungry all the time. I lost a lot of weight because it seemed I never had enough time to eat my fill, what with chores and school and work, but for my brother, maintaining his weight became an obsession. Hard work doesn't make you bulk up, he discovered; it makes you lean. In a panic, he ordered weight supplements from the back of comic books and the weightlifting magazines he subscribed to, things like Joe Weider's Dynamic Weight Gainer, and orange powders that looked like Tang. He mixed them into water, soda, milk. He was desperate to put on bulk. He was desperate not only to be strong but to appear strong. It was not vanity that propelled his obsession. He understood full well that his survival depended on it.

21

The Fine Art of Denial

When I was an adult and had moved away from home, we used to argue about South Dakota, my father and I.

"People were racist against Asians," I'd say.

"That's not true. There's no racism against Chinese in America today. Look at all the successful and rich Chinese in this country!"

"What about us? What about our dogs? People killed them in the driveway!"

"The hunters mistook them for pheasants. They didn't know it was our house. It was a long driveway."

"It wasn't *that* long!"

But always I'd return to the time some boys had tried to kill my brother. Boys armed with baseball bats and two-by-fours. A dark night. After a high school basketball game.

My father would profess ignorance. "Why didn't Mom tell me about that? She never said anything to me."

"Then you didn't want to know!" I would shout. "You're driving me crazy! You're driving me crazy!" I could repeat this endlessly.

"Then you're crazy!" he'd finish.

If we argued on the phone, I slammed the receiver down. If we argued face to face, I would run from the room in exasperation, my voice turning into an inhuman screech. I'd give up trying to make sense, no longer try to form words.

The last time we argued, we were writing a book together, a book about my grandmother. He had envisioned it as heroic, triumphant, how Nai-nai had saved the family during World War II in China; but I added conflict, the family fights, the bitterness that lingered long after the war had ended, all the elements that I had been taught in college make literature great, the things that make us human. My father couldn't fathom what I was trying to do. "You're a negative person," he concluded.

My father had been raised to believe in the fine art of denial. To save face at all costs. Never to admit weakness or failure or even adversity. The only way to conquer one's problems was to pretend they didn't exist.

If you read traditional family memoirs published in Chinese, you will see that he is not alone. Each book describes the triumphs of a family, the generation that has succeeded, garnered acclaim and wealth, exalted positions, prestigious awards. We honor our parents by describing their loving devotion, their sacrifice and hard work, their willingness to push their children to succeed. In this sense such memoirs are no different from the carved tablets that used to be found in ancestral temples, stories of successful exam candidates and virtuous widows. Nobody writes about the family that dies in a famine, the son who loses the farm during a pestilence, the daughter who shouts madly at her father, the father who disappoints his children.

Sure, Pearl Buck wrote about such things, but she was not Chinese.

My father used to believe that he was the only man who had bad luck. Who stumbled on the path to the American Dream. He used to feel ashamed; he could think of nothing else but the heat in his heart, the pounding in his ears, the rage that shook his bones.

He wanted his children to be strong. He wanted us to be confident. He didn't want us to make his mistakes, so he told us there was no such thing as prejudice so that it would not curtail our expectations for ourselves. He denied the past so that we could have a future unfettered by the weight of an unhappy history. What he had forgotten was that a father cannot mold the world to fit the needs of his offspring, no matter how strong his will.

22 The Lone Apache

One night I heard my brother's motorcycle racing up the driveway, spewing gravel. It was late, I should have been in bed asleep, but I had insomnia and was always awake now. My father was gone to Chicago or there'd have been hell to pay, he'd shout at Jeff for coming home at this hour. But he was gone, so my brother came to my room and stood outside my door.

"You awake?" he whispered. Maybe he didn't even have to say the words. I sensed his presence, got up from my bed, and came into his room.

"I thought I was going to die," my brother said. And then he told me what had happened.

It's a dark night and all the kids are gathered in the parking lot behind the high school. The moon keeps disappearing behind the clouds racing across the sky as though they need to be in Minnesota before daybreak, as though they are being chased. The wind is odd this evening, not spring-like, not moist like most March winds. This one howls like a blizzard, lashes the skin like a whip.

Everyone gathers in the parking lot after the basketball game. There's nothing else to do. The restaurants don't stay open past nine. The bars won't let teenagers in. There's no mall, no McDonald's, no multiplex—this town is too small. So everyone gathers in the blue-white pools of light beneath the three or four street lamps. They clump together, girls with girls, boys with boys, eyeing each other with curiosity. The steady couples have already gone elsewhere. They're necking in the backs of the cars borrowed from their parents, in the cab of their best friend's pickup. Everyone else is standing around in the parking lot. Some of the boys hoot, cupping their hands around their mouths. They hoot to see how the girls will react: will they like it? This sound like a monkey's mating call? A few girls giggle. A few more boys hoot. The girls decide, no, they don't like it, and turn away. The boys stop hooting.

It's exciting for no good reason except that everyone is young and the parents are gone; they have climbed into their cars and are in the process of driving away, back to this or that small town or to their farms. Some people have driven halfway across the state to watch the game. Some people keep the high school schedules taped to their calendars, stuck to their refrigerator doors with magnets, paper-clipped to the cover of their phone book on the kitchen counter, so they'll be sure not to miss any. There's nothing more interesting than high school sports. Watching the games brings back so many memories, what it was like to be young and full of potential, your whole life ahead of you. Your bones didn't ache from sitting on a vibrating tractor seat all day, your knees didn't crack when you bent over a cow in the muddy yard. You drank a lot but you didn't feel like you'd been clocked in the temple with the butt of a gun the next morning. The only thing that reminds you of your youth is watching the young people play.

It's exciting to be sixteen. To feel the blood coursing through your veins, your strong, young, healthy heart pumping all those gallons of red blood through your pulsing, sweating, oily, hairy, hormone-driven body.

My brother is standing with his two best friends, the farm kid and the kid who wishes he had a farm. They are watching the girls on the other side of the parking lot, pretending that they are not watching the girls. They are trying to be cool. My brother has on his new leather jacket, the one he got from the mall in Sioux City, Iowa. No one else has a jacket like this. It goes with his motorcycle. When the girls glance back at my brother and his friends, while pretending not to glance back, they are in fact glancing at my brother. At sixteen, he is very nearly perfect looking. Tall, dark, wavy hair, green eyes, chiseled cheekbones. He's muscular but trim. He looks like a movie star.

Everyone is just standing around like this, wondering what to do next, not yet ready to drive home, unsure where the local keg party is, waiting.

Then the Yankton boys step out of the shadows. They have weapons, the usual kind, baseball bats and two-by-fours. Everyone's got one in the back of his pickup. Just in case. It used to surprise me. Just in case of what? I'd ask. In case I need one, was the usual answer. In New Jersey, on the cul-de-sac behind our house on the Newark-Pompton Turnpike, where the kids didn't have to worry about traffic, impromptu baseball games broke out in the middle of the street every afternoon. Someone would appear with a bat and a ball, or a leather glove and cap, and then more kids would appear, boys and girls, all carrying their bats, their gloves. Wiffle bats, Wiffle balls, softballs, sometimes just stickball. It didn't matter about the implements. Sometimes we didn't even keep score. We just loved the game so much. But in South Dakota, nobody I knew played baseball. The wind made the sport impractical. Yet everyone had a bat, it seemed.

The Yankton boys walk in a pack. They are uncertain of themselves as individuals but together they feel they are more than the sum of their parts. They walk toward my brother, bats in hand.

"Hey," one of them grunts. He's not shouting at first. He's trying out his voice, trying it on for size. How it feels. He decides it feels good. "Hey, gut!"

My brother realizes the boy is talking to him. The three Yankton boys line up before him. They are tall, taller than my brother, who is only six feet. The boys in this part of the country are enormous, the descendants of Vikings, hands like shovels, barrel chests. You've seen these kinds of boys in movies; they're the extras wearing helmets with horns on either side. They are pale in the x-ray light of the street lamps, their skin glowing, their scalps shining beneath their short buzz cuts. Their blue eyes glitter.

My brother feels the excitement in the crowd. There's going to be a fight.

Jeff doesn't even pray. There's no time. He is sizing things up. His fighting instincts come first, they're automatic. Nothing else crowds his mind; he's flipped into survival mode. Only he's not going to survive. He can tell this at a glance. There are three white boys, armed with bats and boards, and they are huge. They don't look like boys. They have such broad, muscled shoulders that they no longer have necks. My brother has tried to achieve this look with weight training; he's ordered a special neck machine from Sears just for this purpose. I've watched him use it. It looks like something from a medieval torture chamber, something invented during the Spanish Inquisition. He dons a cap of nylon ropes, fastens a woven strap under his chin. The headpiece is attached to a metal chain, which is attached in turn to a pulley and then to a metal cord that runs to a vertical bar, upon which he may affix any number of weights. He then leans forward, leading with his chin, and the veins on his neck bulge and struggle, his skin turns crimson, then purple, then a deep blue. My mother cries: Stop, stop! Every time she catches him working out on the neck machine, she can't stop her tears. He doesn't listen to her. He doesn't listen to me.

Yet his neck remains as delicate as a swan's.

My brother doesn't understand it at the time, but he has committed the biggest sin possible in our part of South Dakota. Indian boys don't go watching white girls play basketball. Not unless they have a relative playing on one of the teams. Not unless they come in a group and stay with that group. They certainly don't wander out into the middle of a parking lot on a dark night, mingling with the white kids.

"Hey, you!" one of the white boys calls out unnecessarily. He rubs his club-fingered hand up and down the bat. "You!"

There's only a split second in which to act. My brother glances around and sees that his friends have disappeared into the crowd of white kids gathering to watch the fight. They were his last hope, the only plan he could think of, the three of them fighting bare-fisted against these three boys with weapons, but now he's alone, and he can see by the way the light from the street lamps reflects off the teeth of the crowd gathering around him that his classmates are ready to be entertained. Girls are smiling. Boys too. My brother realizes he is going to die. But he puts up his fists anyway.

And then suddenly there is a body beside him, a voice. "C'mon, Chai, we can take 'em."

It's not one of his friends. It's another kid, a year behind my brother in school. Short but stocky, shaped like a wrestler, lean, no neck. His older brother's one of the pretty boys in school, preppy, button-down shirts from Ralph Lauren, Dockers, but this kid is all attitude, ripped T-shirts and ragged jeans. He's already been held back once. Now he's got his fists up and he's hopping from foot to foot behind my brother. He's not much of a fighter, but he's one of those kids who likes to rebel.

My brother's not optimistic, but two against three is better than three beating one boy to death quickly and savagely with their baseball bats. He swallows and faces the Yankton boys.

But now the white boys are nervous. They're confused. What's the white boy doing with the Indian? They squint into the crowd. They're trying to decide whether anyone else is likely to switch sides like that. What if the crowd switches sides? The crowd presses closer, excited by the change in events. The boys are no longer certain. They're a long way from Yankton and they can't judge what people here are liable to do.

"Ha!" One of the boys coughs up a loogie and spits the phlegm noisily onto the asphalt. "He ain't worth it," he says.

The other boys make loud sounds of concurrence. They laugh loudly to mask their fear. You can't tell with the Indians what's gonna happen next. They fight dirty. Who knew he had a white friend? You just couldn't tell what those guts were up to. They're sneaky like that.

My brother watches as the Yankton boys turn and head back to their own pickups on the edge of the lot. He doesn't relax until the crowd has begun to disperse, couples pairing off, photocopies of directions to the kegger being passed from hand to hand. Once the crowd has decided there's not going to be a fight, my brother believes it too. He can breathe again. He knows he's going to live.

His friends return, smiling. They want to congratulate my brother. He feels their hands slapping his back, through his leather coat. He feels their sweaty palms as clearly as though he were naked. He can feel their sweat directly against his skin.

When my brother is older, in college—or maybe I'm the one in college and that's why Jeff is by himself—he is sitting at the counter of one of the local steak-and-burger joints, sipping a Coke, when an Indian slips onto the seat beside him. They exchange a few words, and then comes the question, asked almost shyly, the question that will determine the rest of the conversation, how long it will be, its subject. Indians always ask each other this question, the way Chinese greet each other by asking, "Have you eaten yet?" Like a secret handshake, it opens the door to the brotherhood.

The Indian asks, "So, what tribe are you?"

My brother hesitates a moment. He's been asked this question a hundred times before. He's used to the shock, then the disappointment when he tells them the answer. He's used to the door of the brotherhood cracking open just a peek and then slamming shut in his face. My brother is tired. This night he replies, "Apache."

"Apache! What are you doing up here?"

"I came up from Texas," my brother says, thinking fast, "just to see what it's like."

"I'm Lakota Sioux." The young man is rubbing his hands on the knees of his jeans, he's so excited. A bona fide Apache. The warrior of warriors. Apaches are the coolest Indians in the world. Everybody knows this. They were never defeated by the white man. Their leader Geronimo kept the U.S. government at bay for decades, leading a guerilla war from Mexico. My brother knows this because he's seen the movies, all the Westerns we used to watch as kids in New Jersey. The 4:30 movie special on Channel 7, five days a week. We've seen Geronimo leap to his death off the cliffs of the Grand Canyon rather than be taken alive by the cavalry. "Geronimooooo," he shouts as he spirals through the air. The cavalry take aim, shooting madly, their bullets ricocheting wildly off the rocks. But they can't hit Geronimo. He sails to the river below, his body never recovered. That's why parachutists shout "Geronimo!" when they leap from planes. It's an exclamation of bravery.

This story is nothing we've been taught in school. School teaches nothing about the Indians. It's a story we learned from watching TV, and every kid in our school knew it. There used to be fights in our backyard between my brother's friends about who got to be the Indians, who had to be the cowboys—it was unimaginable to us in those days that one could exist without the other. There had to be a fight, after all. There had to be a war. What else was there to play? Sometimes they'd decide paper-scissors-rock. Sometimes the bigger boys would just grab the rifles and the plastic feather headdresses that used to be sold in four-packs in the toy aisle of the grocery store. Losers got stuck with six-shooters and foil-covered sheriff's stars to pin on their shirts.

Unfortunately, none of the Geronimo story we learned in New Jersey was true. It was just a screenwriter's fantasy. In real life, Geronimo surrendered to the Feds after he realized his people were starving to death with no land to call their own. He agreed to move to a reservation but was instead imprisoned in Florida and sentenced to hard labor. He died in poverty in Oklahoma territory, after failing to learn how to farm.

My brother, however, is confident in his Hollywood history. This is the story he tells the Lakota boy, at any rate, the story of the heroic, triumphant, undefeated Apaches and the flummoxed, defeated, frustrated federal agents sent to assassinate the great Geronimo. The Lakota boy hasn't heard the real story of the Apache, either, or maybe he doesn't care. Maybe he likes this version better. And my brother tells it well, so that they can both see the battle, hear the gunshots, hear Geronimo's last, echoing cry as he plunges through the Grand Canyon.

"And they never found his body," my brother adds at the end.

They laugh together. It's a great story, a great ending. It's the way history should have happened. Whatever Jewish immigrant screenwriter dreamed up this version, he should be congratulated.

"That's cool." The Lakota boy nods, drawing on a cigarette. My brother watches the smoke spiral into the air between them. "So, your grandpa tell you this story, huh?"

"Not exactly," my brother begins. He's going to launch into another story. Maybe this time he could invent a warrior grandfather. A witness to history. A participant. That would be better. That would be great.

"I'm gonna tell everybody I met you here." The Lakota boy is squinting into the smoky dark air. "Any more of your tribe coming up? I can show you around. We can go to the Hills."

The Lakota boy says he'd like to introduce my brother to the elders, they should hear this story, too. It would make them happy. Geronimo's victory.

The music from the jukebox seems to grow louder in my brother's ears. It's a country-and-western song. It's always a country-and-western song. The sound could drive you mad here if you let it. The air is too thick with smoke. There's a pool game going on in the back of the bar. Some men are arguing, their voices sloppy with drink.

My brother's stomach is dropping away. It could be he who's plunged off a cliff wall. He feels it now with certainty. He's crossed a line without meaning to. It's just that he's been so lonely, he's neither a cowboy nor an Indian and it had felt so good to belong somewhere. To have a tribe. But there's no tribe here for my brother. And he begins to understand that he's done something wrong. Something even cruel, perhaps.

"Actually, I'm not an Apache." My brother hears his voice emerging from his mouth. The words float up from his throat and slip out between his teeth before he can stop them. "I'm half Chinese."

The Lakota boy looks shocked, and then disappointed.

"Sorry," my brother says.

"Oh."

Then he laughs and my brother laughs. It's funny after all. But then there's nothing more to say.

The music grows very loud in my brother's ears until he can't distinguish the woman's nasal voice from the twanging guitar. The sounds vibrate together, humming in his inner ear. He feels bees have settled in his skull. Even his bones are buzzing.

The Indian boy gets up and joins a new group of Indians who have come in the door.

My brother sits alone, watching the cowboys and the Indians on their opposite sides of the room, each group in its own place. Then he gets up and goes home.

23

My Mother's Irish Gang

By the time I was seventeen, I had fallen into despair. I was only a year away from college, a year away from escaping, but I was so tired. I kept a bottle of extra-strength Tylenol in my dresser drawer. My way out, I called it. If things got any worse, I planned to take them all and kill myself. At the time, I didn't think practically about backup plans, what to do if I started throwing up the Tylenol, for example. I didn't think about the possibility of surviving and having to live with severe liver damage. When you're young, it's hard to plan for all eventualities. It was enough to know I had the pills. Just in case.

One of my brother's friends lost his virginity and bragged to anyone who would listen. The dark and starry night in the back of his pickup. The six-pack of beer he and the girl had consumed.

"I didn't use protection," the boy recalled, giggling. "Loretta didn't mind."

Loretta was his first cousin.

Things like this made me sick. They made me want to flee immediately, on foot if necessary. Well, of course on foot because I didn't have a car, and there was no public transportation here, no buses no cabs no trains no airport. I took up jogging, running circles in our back brome field. I got the satisfaction of feeling as though I had taken flight, even though there was nowhere to go.

A year left. Three hundred sixty-five and a quarter days.

I wouldn't have made it if not for my mother. She always encouraged me, told me to aim high and never apologize for having ambition and aspirations. In our town girls were supposed to act dumb, get poor grades, and let the boys compete in the math contests. My mother told me I shouldn't accept second-best, and every time I won an academic prize she would celebrate, buy me a new outfit, tell everyone in town what her daughter had done.

She taught me how to develop film—both color and black-and-white—paid for me to attend a professional photography school so that I could learn how to light individuals and groups appropriately for every shade of skin. She gave me all the responsibilities of an adult in our business—I learned to take pictures, keep our accounts, file the quarterly income tax report.

Sometimes when we went on wedding shoots together, I would be setting up the lights, my mother would be checking the altar for good angles, when one of the women in the wedding party would approach me.

"Where's the photographer? I don't see him," she'd say.

"She's already here," I'd say proudly and point to my mother.

Most people would not have guessed how tough my mother was just from looking at her. She appeared very soft, very kind, inherently feminine. She smiled easily. She was very slender and beautiful, with a natural grace that I did not inherit. She liked colorful dresses in flowery prints and always wore a pair of heels. She had unusually long arms for a woman of her height, and once, after reading that the span of one's arms should be the same as one's height, my brother and I took to measuring all of us, twice, just to be sure we hadn't made a mistake. We discovered that with arms of her length, our mother should have been six feet four inches tall, but in fact she was just a little under five eight. She also had long tapered fingers and exceptionally bony, long wrists, perfect for bracelets, which she always wore, several at a time, including a cream-colored circle carved from Bakelite that had been given to her by her maternal grandmother, who'd insisted it was Chinese ivory. It was intricately embellished with chrysanthemums and peonies, various vines and leaves, and an imaginary flower with pointy petals. When my mother gestured with her hands, which she did frequently, her bracelets jangled together like chimes.

Because she had been obliged to work very hard from a young age, eight or nine years old, the veins on her hands stood up from the skin, always at attention. She thought her long hands looked unattractive and wore many rings on her fingers to draw attention away from the veins. As a result, her hands sparkled all the time.

Some people mistook these traits for weakness, her prettiness, her womanliness, but my mother had always been very brave. There wasn't a weak bone in her body.

When she was four and a half years old, she awoke to the sound of screams and loud thumping sounds outside her room. She jumped from her bed and stumbled into the hallway to find her father, drunk and reeling, trying to strangle her mother. She took off in a run to the closest neighbors who were known to have a phone in those days, even though they lived a quarter-mile away. When she arrived, however, the neighbors refused to call the sheriff.

It was 1938, after all, and a fight between a man and his wife was considered no one's business but their own.

The next day my grandparents came by to pick up my mother from the neighbors' house, and everyone acted, to my mother's astonishment, as though this were the most normal thing in the world, as though nothing had happened at all. My grandfather later apologized profusely to my grandmother for his behavior and promised he'd never do it again. My grandmother, pregnant with her third child, wanted to believe him. And in fact, he did keep his promise for the next six or seven months.

Later, as my mother's family grew to include six, then seven, then eight children, as they moved from town to town (twenty-seven times before my mother graduated from high school), as the excuses grew, and as her mother grew despairing when the ministers and the priests refused to intervene because it was the wife's duty to be a helpmeet, when the police or the sheriff picked up my grandfather from a drunken brawl at a bar or the VFW and brought him home, admonishing my grandmother, "Keep a better eye on your husband, Ma'am," my mother came to realize that sometimes there was no one else to turn to in the world, that it would be between her and God alone to protect her younger siblings from her father's rages and her mother's despair. She accepted this responsibility at a young age, and once, when she was sick with the flu and armed only with a yardstick and a lot of attitude, she managed to physically throw out of the house a drunken sailor her father had brought home, picking him up by the back of his shirt and running him out the front door and down the front steps, much to the astonishment of both men. When my grandfather, in a drunken fit, cooked the children's rabbits one summer's day, she intervened again. Her father knocked one of her teeth out, but by the end of the fight none of the children had to eat their pets. Over the years she fought and fought, working to provide scholarships for her sisters and brother, special art lessons or music and dance classes, a warm coat here and there, dresses for the prom, a job in the library for a sister, an internship with Walt Disney for her beloved only brother. She did what she could to protect her family, knowing the law was not going to do a thing.

And in the end, thanks in no small part to her efforts, all of her younger siblings survived.

My mother was a fighter, all right.

In our town in South Dakota, my mother understood our problem quite well: we lacked allies. She also understood that the Native Americans were not the only people in town who belonged to tribes. The whites were hardly unified—they saw themselves as their forebears must have, as Norwegians, Swedes, Germans, Irish. They weren't Christians but Methodists, Lutherans, Baptists, Catholics. People tended to marry within their tribe, even if that meant marrying a cousin. And so my mother decided to use her own background to our family's advantage and formed an Irish gang.

Through the photography studio she opened, she put her background in art to practical use, shooting family portraits, senior pictures, Little League games, weddings. She also joined the local

Chamber of Commerce and a businesswomen's association. She was gathering allies for herself. As a white woman, she alone among us could fit in here, and she decided to use this to our advantage.

She found the first member of her gang through my job with the newspaper. She'd persuaded the editor of the town paper to let me write a weekly feature story. Basically, I'd interview someone in our community and write a little story about that person's life. It wasn't exactly Pentagon Papers material, but readers liked my features and so the editor kept me on. I had grown terribly shy over the years and it took a supreme effort on my part to approach people and ask for an interview, but since I got paid for each story—extra for a photograph—I learned to overcome my shyness. Usually I'd stare at my notebook as I asked my questions, barely lifting my head and scribbling notes furiously. My mother drove me around to my interview sites, and when I'd finished I would dash away to her waiting Jeep, waving a little in adieu without turning to look back.

There was a restaurant called the Kerry House at the juncture of two state highways. It was really in the middle of nowhere, to my eyes, rising out of the corn and soybean fields, a lone building with a single-pump gas station out front. It was the kind of lonely squat building that made one think of a ghost town, a settlement that had been started by someone optimistic, then abandoned as fortunes went south, but the Kerry House wasn't as lonely as it looked. You could see it from the highway, so it did a fair amount of trucking business, along with local business owners' noontime lunches. The owner, I was told, also did a good business in Norwegian holidays, preparing all the traditional foods, from lutefisk to *lefse*, even decorating the interior with crepe-paper streamers in the national colors of Norway. What caught my eye, however, was the long line of Gaelic painted across the side of the building. I liked the idea that someone had been so bold as to promote a foreign language in our town.

After I called to set up an interview, I discovered that the owner was indeed an Irish immigrant, a woman named Mary Imelda Lynch. Decades earlier she'd left her homeland to go to school at Mount St. Mary's College in Sioux City, Iowa, met a farmer from South Dakota, and married him. She'd never been back to Ireland.

Some people in town looked askance at Imelda Lynch, because after her youngest daughter had died in a car accident she'd stopped going to church, renounced her faith in God, and was rumored on occasion to berate the pope.

My mother got along with her from the start. I was supposed to be conducting the interview, but soon it was my mother who was asking all the questions. She had driven me to the Kerry House. Now she began to interrupt me as I asked Imelda questions about her business, and soon she and Imelda were talking animatedly as though I weren't there at all. It was kind of humiliating for me as a cub reporter, but to be fair my mother had been lonely all these years and she'd finally found someone who laughed at all her jokes.

Imelda herself had a sardonic sense of humor, a cutting edge to her observations, and a rather cynical view of the world. She didn't give a damn about small-town politics and said what she thought outright. My mother loved these qualities in her new friend, even if at first glance the two women seemed to have little in common. Imelda was a farmer's wife and had lived in small towns all her life. She didn't like to travel, wasn't particularly interested in art, and had no interest in books or museums or any of the things that had defined my mother's life before South Dakota. Imelda even looked like my mother's opposite—whereas my mother was tall, blonde, and slender, Imelda was petite, brunette, and shapely. Personally, I found Imelda Lynch a little intimidating, with her sharp tongue and sarcastic wit, her tendency to squint before she smiled, and the way she stared at me unabashedly, a little annoyed, as though she expected me to sprout wings and buzz about her head like a pesky fly. But my mother was enthralled by what she called Imelda's "Gaelic charm."

My mother always had a soft spot in her heart for the Irish. Not the Irish as TV shows and movies in those days portrayed them: bucolic folk surrounded by green fields, trilling to the joys of their shared bar of Irish Spring, or superstitious people who believed in the Lucky Charms leprechaun.

No, my mother loved the Irish because they were tough. They were treated like crap when they came to America and they fought back. They had survived famine, poverty, prejudice, and even assimilation. She liked the tough Irish nuns of her childhood in Indiana and delighted in telling Jeff and me stories about "beloved Sister Berarda," who had rescued my mother from schoolyard bullies when she was in seventh grade. By that time my mother had had every childhood illness known to man, one after the after. She'd been quarantined for months, and when she returned to school she was ghostly thin, pale, and weak. Immediately the other kids had tried to pounce upon her in the playground, but then dear Sister Berarda had seen them and come gliding out of the school, her black robes trailing behind her in the wind, a raised yardstick in one hand. She'd grabbed those nasty boys by the scruff of their necks, dragged them back into the classroom, and beaten them with her ruler until they saw the error of their ways. My mother had heard their cries even through the closed windows.

"Now, that was a strong woman!" my mother said. Educated, authoritative, and tough.

As for myself, I had found this story terrifying as a child. When my mother had tried to enroll me in Catholic school immediately after we moved to New Jersey, I lasted exactly four days. Public kindergarten had been grand in California. We sang songs every day, learned nonviolent methods of conflict resolution, and conducted dances under a surplus parachute, the kind that the military used to donate to public schools, so that almost everyone I've met in my generation, on both coasts, can remember those P.E. classes conducted under parachutes. (Was it a national policy to supply public schools with army surplus from the Vietnam War?) But in Catholic school, the nuns would have none of that nonsense. Instead we learned good competitive games like kickball and tag and dodge ball. The more physical contact, the better. I remember cringing in fear the first time I was "it" and was made to stand in the middle of the circle of taunting first-graders as they tried to hit me with the large, red rubber "dodge" ball. I kept running around and around, refusing to try to catch the ball, until one of the nuns grabbed me by the shoulders with her talons and refused to let me go. "Don't be afraid of the ball," she hissed. "Don't be a sissy!"

On the fourth and final day of my Catholic school experiment, the nun who taught my class backhanded a boy with a broken arm because he'd worked ahead in our reading workbook. I was too terrified to speak. I myself had considered working ahead—the book was too easy—and had even asked my mother if that would be okay. My mother had said, Yes, of course, but at the last minute I'd decided against it. Sister Mary had seemed pretty adamant that we only do four pages. Now Sister Mary was standing over the weeping boy she had slapped. As he sobbed, "But my mommy said I could," she mocked him, imitating his crying voice, "But Mommy isn't here, is she?" I thought she would whip out her broomstick at any moment. I was so scared after this episode that I couldn't pee for the rest of the day—through two bathroom breaks, lunch, and recess—and ended up running all the way home in tears, fleeing from the brick two-story schoolhouse as soon as the afternoon bell rang at three, not even waiting for the nun to dismiss us, but simply rising from my seat and running as fast as my short legs could carry me.

After that, my mother enrolled me in public school.

Still, she never lost her faith in nuns.

She herself was Irish on her mother's side, although the exact provenance was unknown. Her grandmother had been orphaned at the age of four, after her parents had tried to homestead in Kentucky in the 1880s. They'd had to ford a river in their tiny covered wagon and had nearly been swept downstream. First her father had jumped off the buckboard, grabbing hold of the horses' reins, and then her mother, swimming alongside the horses as they crossed the raging river. My mother's grandmother, Lenore, had been placed in charge of the family's single treasure—a tiny brown Irish teapot that was all that had survived from an early journey across the Atlantic Ocean. They all made it across the river, the teapot intact, but Lenore's father soon developed a cough, then consumption, and died. Lenore's mother lasted through most of the winter, setting traps in the woods, chopping wood for the fire, trying to be a real pioneer woman, but she too had weak lungs and eventually succumbed. Lenore was sent to live with another couple in Kentucky, who insisted she call them "Uncle" and "Aunt" but forced her to leave school at the age of eight to earn her keep as the family servant. She left that house after she became pregnant at the age of fifteen. She liked to say that the father of her baby was the family's son, who was about her age and who had fallen in love with her, but it might also have been her "Uncle," who had started molesting her the year before.

My mother's grandmother never received much of a formal education, but she was a hard worker, eventually ran many businesses, among them a restaurant and a laundry, married several times, divorced several times, and could say with pride at the end of her life that she'd never put up with any foolishness from any man and had earned her own keep in the world.

Some people might have seen Lenore's story as tragic, but my mother had always admired her Irish grandmother. "She was a real survivor," my mother used to say with pride. "My grandmother, she really knew how to work."

I remember one of the parties my mother threw at Imelda's Kerry House. A Hawaiian luau in February. We hadn't seen the ground since the first heavy snowfall in November. The drifts had turned into small mountains on our property and the wind chill was so severe that year that the state highway patrol actually banned driving on several occasions. That way, if anyone ran off the road and went into the ditch, the troopers wouldn't be required to go out in the cold and tow them out.

"Let's have a luau, Imelda!" my mother said, after we drove out to the Kerry House one afternoon with our egg delivery.

"All right," Imelda agreed. "What's a luau?"

It was up to my mother to explain the basics to her new group of friends, which by now, in addition to Imelda and her husband, included a Democratic state senator who'd lost his post after redistricting and his wife, a few local business owners my mother had met after joining the Chamber of Commerce, several farm families, a former missionary and her husband, two priests, and the lone nun from our church. They were all Irish Catholic except for the missionary, who was Mormon (although the circle eventually expanded to include several Norwegian Protestants as well).

When my mother announced her plan, she discovered that the missionary had lived in Hawaii for some time and actually knew how to hula.

"Wonderful!" my mother exclaimed. "You can teach the rest of us."

Then she set about making the decorations. She and I strung several dozen leis together out of plastic flowers. We found novelty hula skirts at a drugstore and bought them for guests. She sewed loose Hawaiian shirts that could be pulled over sweaters. Then she started on the big set pieces.

I remember her trying to explain to the man behind the counter at the Ben Franklin's.

"I'm making a palm tree—"

"A what tree?" the man exclaimed.

"Yes, a Hawaiian palm tree for my luau." My mother gestured for me to haul her tree over. It was more than six feet tall, something she had constructed out of papier-mâché and cardboard tubing, construction paper and poster paint. It was heavy, unwieldy, and had lost one of its fronds to a particularly tall snow drift that we'd stumbled into as my mother and I carried it from her studio to the five-and-dime, me at the base, she at the tip.

The man behind the counter lifted his eyebrows.

"I thought you'd be able to think up some solution for me," my mother said, smiling at him. Now that she was a blonde, she was not above flirting to get her way. "You see, I need some sort of pot to anchor it. Or it tips over."

I demonstrated, allowing the palm to stand on its own and then fall over into my arms.

"I was thinking, maybe one of your flower pots, or these wicker baskets. What do you think if I fill them up with rocks? Are they strong enough?" My mother inspected a series of plastic flowers set into ceramic pots at the end of an aisle.

The man smiled now at my mother. Pushing his round glasses back up his nose, slicking his hair back with one hand, he emerged from behind the counter.

"Now, now, those won't do any good at all. Let me see what you've got here." The man grasped the palm tree, weighing it in his hands.

"Why, let me tell you what I can do. I can set this into a base for you. I've got some cement in the back. It won't be a problem at all."

"Oh, could you do that for me? I just knew you'd think of something!" My mother smiled at the man gratefully.

"No problem. No problem at all . . ." he hesitated and then he added, as though trying it on his tongue, tasting it, "*Carolyn.*"

"You're wonderful!" my mother proclaimed, and the man actually blushed.

Then she and I were out the door and trotting back through the snow to our photography studio around the corner.

I couldn't help but admire my mother at these moments. She'd really turned this blonde thing into an art form.

The luau was a grand success, and she soon followed it with other theme parties. She'd bring props from the photography studio to the Kerry House and create a new atmosphere each time. Casablanca with wicker chairs, fedoras, and trench coats, Ode to Spring with giant flowers she made by stretching dyed nylons over petals made from coat hangers, the Roaring Twenties with flapper dresses, feathered fans, and fancy headbands.

In the spring, when the weather improved, she and my father threw big parties on the farm. They hadn't entertained at all after my father left his job at the university, but now they returned to form. And the circle of their friends expanded; even a few professors dared to come over now.

My parents loved these big, dramatic gatherings. My mother cooked elaborate, multicourse buffets that she arranged according to color, announcing, "Red! I need something red!" before quickly adding bell peppers to a salad or a radish rose to a platter, so that every dish was pleasing to the eye as well as the palate. My father loved to entertain with his exciting stories. He mixed the drinks and mingled with the guests, all the farmers and local politicians, priests and professors and businesspeople, who gathered at our house.

One time he ordered Chinese kites from a catalog and had everyone running in the brome field, flying phoenixes and giant moths, butterflies and one spectacular long green dragon. My mother handed out jars of soapy water to the priests and nun, and soon they were blowing bubbles on our bluegrass. My brother and I set off fireworks in the evening. Everyone agreed there had never been such a party!

My parents were elegant and dramatic in a way that made them stand out wherever they went. This was true even in New York. When we first moved to South Dakota, I used to wish they knew how to blend in better. I wished that they could make themselves look like my classmates' parents, like people who belonged. It was only much later, when I was older and had moved away, that I began to appreciate the aplomb with which my parents had carried themselves.

For the St. Patrick's Day dance at the local Catholic church hall, my mother dressed in a black beaded gown, my father in a slim tailored suit, a yellow silk handkerchief folded into a triangle in his breast pocket. Although they were running late, I made them pose for a picture before they left.

Sometimes I'd stare at this photo of my parents at night when I couldn't sleep. I'd turn my desk lamp on, placing a scarf over the shade so that no one would notice the light coming from my room. Because my mother liked to wear heels, my father always stood perfectly erect beside her. They were very nearly the same height, and he didn't want to appear short. I liked this picture because they looked so happy in it, with the excited, expectant expressions they wore when they were going out. I wished they could look like this at home, too. Like a couple who didn't have a care in the world.

Between my mother's photography studio and the parties, my parents eventually came to have a place in our town. They had a circle of friends now. My father began to get involved in local politics. Drawing upon the support of my mother's Irish gang, he held fund-raisers for a young man named Tom Daschle and helped him to get elected to the U.S. Senate. Later, my parents would help a local lawyer named Tim Johnson run for Congress. They liked progressive candidates who supported education and wanted to bring new business to the state. What my father hadn't been able to achieve at the university, he could now do through politics. He grew happier, excited, and he became a campaign advisor to candidates in other states who'd heard about his successes with Daschle and Johnson and wanted his advice, including John Glenn and Richard Gephardt. And in 1988, my father fulfilled a personal dream, becoming a state-elected delegate to the Democratic Convention in Atlanta.

But *although things improved* for my parents, there were still many signs that people did not want my brother and me in their community.

A girl's mother tried to get me kicked off the school's National History Day team. She said I didn't deserve to go to Washington, D.C., because I'd already been there, and insisted her daughter be put on the team in my place. It made no logical sense, but the woman was adamant. She followed my mother and me through the church parking lot, shouting at us. In the end, she wasn't allowed to change the competition's rules—I had scored higher than her daughter; therefore I was on the team. Still, I didn't hang out with my other teammates once we made it to the capital. I felt betrayed, and instead tagged along with the team from another town.

Then my brother was attacked during wrestling practice. He had been recruited to join the varsity team that fall, although my brother had never before wrestled on the team. Jeff was very athletic, naturally gifted, and he was good at almost every sport he tried. All the gym teachers knew this. My parents were vehemently opposed to team sports, as they felt such activities suppressed the will of the individual. They were fond of pointing out how all fascist and communist regimes relied heavily on sports victories to instill a spirit of nationalism in their people. Many coaches still tried to recruit my brother. They'd started calling the summer before his freshman year, but always my parents had refused to let him join. The wrestling coach wouldn't give up. He was used to winning, and he would do what it took to get any player he felt he needed.

Wrestling was the most prestigious sport in our school and in our part of South Dakota. It seemed to be the only sport we could win at. The Indians could beat the white boys at basketball, and in football our team never had much depth. In wrestling, however, we'd taken the state championship for nearly five years in a row and the coach wasn't about to lose this year. Before wrestling tournaments, all classes were canceled and we held enormous pep rallies in the gym. Anyone who didn't attend and cheer was suspended for three days. Teachers paced at the edges of the bleachers, watching us, just to enforce this rule.

They insisted it was essential that we show "school spirit" in order to become well-rounded individuals. Personally, I thought my parents were right about the fascist tendencies.

My brother begged my parents so persistently to let him join the wrestling team that they finally relented.

One afternoon during practice, while the coach was out of the gym, two boys attacked my brother on the mats. He managed to wrestle them both at the same time, but while he was in a full bridge extension, his back arched, his ribcage in the air, a third boy climbed up on the bleachers and jumped down onto Jeff's chest. The coach returned before anything more could happen, but the damage was done. Jeff was taken to the hospital. Tests showed his diaphragm had been torn. His wrestling days were over.

The school paid his medical bills, but for the rest of the year he had problems with his GI tract. Swallowing was difficult, and sometimes he could not digest food properly. It could have been much worse, of course, and my mother was thankful that he hadn't been permanently disabled. She had us say a full rosary together to thank God for his protection, but I worried about my brother constantly. I wanted us to leave. Abandon our house and farm. Declare bankruptcy if we had to. Who cares? I thought. Let's just get out of here.

Meanwhile, boys and girls at school still asked me what was wrong with my appearance. "Why is your face so fat and your body so thin? Is it because you're Chinese?" Why was my nose so flat? Why was my hair so straight? I had permed my hair again, but they remembered what it had looked like. I began to think there really was something the matter with how I looked.

My beloved math teacher, who didn't have a prejudiced bone in his body, had a heart attack and disappeared for most of the year to recover from quadruple bypass surgery.

My drama teacher, who'd surprised everyone one year by casting me, a white boy, and a Lakota boy in a romantic comedy, dropped dead of heart failure.

I felt completely alone.

I thought about taking all that Tylenol. Eight months to go. Seven. Six. Five.

The year I turned seventeen men still drove by our house shooting when the weather permitted. My dog, Ernestine, was killed when a pickup truck left the road, chased her into our field, struck her, then backed up over her head. We found the truck's tire tracks in the mud beside her body. Another dog was shot in our driveway, a puppy that my brother had bought for my mother. It was a sweet little mutt, very trusting. My mother had loved him. I think he lived only three or four months. Afterward, my brother regretted buying him at all. After another of our dogs was shot, it managed to drag itself from the driveway to the lawn and then to the ditch. We followed the trail of blood to find its body. I don't even remember this dog's name. After a while, I began to grow numb. Bandi, Shao Gou, Mozart. All shot and killed. I can barely recall their colors, and I've completely forgotten their faces. My mother and brother loved dogs. They always had to replace one after it was killed, but I wished they wouldn't.

24

China's Revolutions

It was China that changed my life and gave me the perspective I needed to regain my confidence.

After I graduated from high school, my father and I took a trip to China for a family reunion. For him it was an emotionally taxing experience, particularly when he discovered that his mother's family was now living in poverty. He remembered his uncles and their children as they had lived before the 1949 revolution—as wealthy physicians with refined tastes. Now they were living in a crowded Beijing apartment with bare walls, rickety wooden furniture, a lone electric fan whirring in the corner to disperse the heat. I, however, had no memories with which to compare the present. I hadn't known our relatives when they were rich, so it didn't upset me now that they were poor. After our years on the farm, "rich" was a purely abstract concept.

I was thrilled to see the Great Wall, the exquisite Temple of Heaven and Summer Palace, the streets thronged with peasants selling their produce—watermelons, tomatoes, mustard greens, pickled peppers, and bok choy piled high in mounds. New private entrepreneurs were opening their stands, selling clothing and small consumer goods. A sense of excitement was in the air, and best of all, nobody stared at me.

I resolved that I would return to China. At Grinnell College in Iowa, I studied Chinese five hours a day, every day, reciting over and over the four tones: high, rising, falling then rising, and falling. The tone chart sounded something like this: Ma, Ma? Maaah, Ma! Ba, Ba? Baaah, Ba! Ta, Ta? Taaah, Ta! And if my three roommates were at all annoyed freshman year, I couldn't hear them complain with my earphones on. Only later did I discover that my entire floor had learned the four Chinese tones from my constant repetitions, when they surprised me by reciting them to me, over and over, in a kind of a New Age carol.

Finally, my junior year, I was ready to attend a study-abroad program in Nanjing. Oddly enough, it was in China that I discovered the liberal intellectual atmosphere I had been longing for. It was 1988, and students at the universities were actively involved in pro-democracy demonstrations. China in the late '80s was very different from the China of today. People were still very startled to see foreigners after their decades of isolation under Mao, and they would stop whatever they were doing to stare at my fellow American classmates. Some young Chinese men would react to the foreigners in their midst with hostility or derision, and they would follow white people down the street, calling out "Hello? Hello?" in an aggressive manner. In this respect, Nanjing reminded me a little of South Dakota.

But more people reacted to the new foreign presence in their midst with enthusiasm. Foreign-language schools were popping up all over the city, as Chinese wanted to interact with the world. I found a job in a night school teaching English to university students trying to get in extra speaking practice, lawyers, businesspeople, models, and retirees. I was paid less than the white students who were hired to teach because the Chinese director of the school told me that I was "not a real American." He assumed that because I was Chinese American, I must have had a Chinese accent when I spoke English. Ironically, some of the teachers he had hired were European and could barely speak English themselves, and one of my classmates had a very thick Texas accent; the director assumed they had standard accents because they were white. But even this kind of prejudice was waning—the head of the English program at Nanjing Normal University hired me, over many other white candidates, to record a series of English-language tapes that would be used to train teachers at colleges all over China. "Your American accent," he said, "is very clear and easy to understand." I had never felt so proud.

Everywhere I went, people were throwing off the intellectual shackles they'd been forced to wear under Mao. New magazines, filled with articles about the world, reviews of movies that would never be shown in China, book reviews, interviews with intellectuals and movie stars, businesspeople and activists, appeared in the private stands of the free markets. Poorly dubbed Western movies were shown in rented rooms of universities or factory work units, and tickets were sold to the public—all privately, by word of mouth, no need to involve the government—so that everyone could see what the rest of the world was watching.

That December, student demonstrations erupted across Nanjing. The first riot occurred at a Christmas Eve party at one of the engineering colleges. The world press widely reported the event as a spontaneous racist outburst after a Chinese security guard refused to allow an African graduate student to enter with his Chinese girlfriend. Supposedly, the security guard was beaten and Chinese "students" then attacked the African student dormitories, shattering windows, breaking into rooms, and throwing rocks at the fleeing foreign students. In fact, the situation was even more complicated. Two white American students had been warned in advance by Chinese administrators at the college not to attend the dance. They were told that something was going to happen. The African students, who were all on government scholarships, had been staging a series of protests at the school in the weeks before the riot. They had discovered that certain administrators were withholding their scholarship funds and speculating with the money for private gain. The African students held sit-ins and other demonstrations in administrative offices to try to force the corrupt officials to return their scholarship money. It was widely believed that a few of these corrupt officials planned the riot at the Christmas Eve party in order to intimidate the African students and keep them from protesting again. If so, this plan backfired.

Some two hundred thugs had been hired to pose as students and destroy the Africans' dormitories. But other Chinese students witnessed the event and clearly recognized that the thugs were not students. They reported this to their classmates and soon tempers were flaring. Before long, the riot had escalated and affected the entire city. If the administrators had hoped to merely intimidate the Africans and keep their collusion under wraps, they were misguided.

Within three days of the Christmas Eve riot, demonstrations erupted all over Nanjing. The BBC and other media reported the "official" version of the riot—that African students had attacked a Chinese security guard, who was reportedly in the hospital, and that Chinese students had attacked the Africans in retaliation. Some racist student groups began parading in the streets calling for all Africans to be expelled from China. Workers joined with them and picketed the city's foreign hotels. In those days, Chinese were not permitted to enter hotels for foreigners and were stopped at the gates by security guards. This infuriated the people, naturally, and so the demonstrators' first stop was Nanjing's tallest skyscraper (at the time), the Jinling Hotel. They carried signs reading, in Chinese, "Foreign Devils, go home! Black Devils, go home!" and "Chinese are second-class citizens in their motherland!" Some of these student groups also circled the dormitories on campus, including the one I was living in, which was open to both Chinese and American students. In those days most dorms were segregated, but Nanjing University had a special policy in which foreign students could room with Chinese, which was one of the reasons I had wanted to study at Nan Da in the first place. Now, we all watched the demonstrators from the windows of our rooms on the upper floors. Hundreds of Chinese swarmed around the dorms below, chanting and waving banners denouncing foreigners. The boy from Texas tried to run out and take a picture. His camera was ripped from his hands and he was carried back into the dormitory. He came running up the steps, scared out of his wits.

Because I generally was mistaken for Chinese, it was decided that I would be the one to try to ride over on my bike to the public telephone booths beside the post office. In those days there were no phone lines capable of calling overseas in the dorm, nor were there cell phones. I would call my parents and instruct them to inform our study-abroad program's American offices that we were trapped in our dorms in the middle of demonstrations and see if they could tell the proper authorities. I would also ask that they try to contact the parents of my classmates to let them know we were all right. Because my father spoke Chinese, we also hoped he could call the Chinese embassy and tell the authorities in Beijing what was going on. The local authorities seemed to have no idea how to handle the situation. The demonstrations were growing in size every day, and the African students had gone into hiding. Some were being protected in locked rooms at the train station. Others had apparently been arrested by the public security bureau and were in "safe keeping" in one of the jails. Rumors abounded that local officials did not want the students to leave the city out of fear that they would head to their embassies in Beijing and the local officials would get into trouble for having allowed the situation to get out of hand.

As I prepared to set off, another American student decided to join me. Doug was a very thin young man, with pale blond hair and limpid blue eyes. He definitely didn't blend in on the streets, but he said he wasn't afraid to venture out with me. He was one of those foreigners whose looks were hard for many Chinese to interpret. He had longish, curly hair, which he wore in a Mel Gibson, Lethal-Weapon-era kind of flip. The hairdo was very popular in the States that year, but most Chinese men in Nanjing sported very short haircuts. As a result, many Chinese did not realize he was male but thought he was a rather homely foreign woman. At first Doug had been embarrassed when he realized everyone thought he was a girl, but now he realized his androgynous looks could come in handy.

We set out together on our bicycles.

The crowds around our dorms had thinned somewhat, but there were still several hundred Chinese young people carrying placards, mostly young men. Fortunately, they were macho enough not to want to beat up on a couple of girls, and let us pass. To their eyes, I looked like a kindly Chinese student escorting her frightened American roommate on an errand. They paid us no mind and we were able to ride out the university gates and down the main streets to the post office.

We were shocked to see that demonstrators now lined the length of Zhong Shan Boulevard, Nanjing's main thoroughfare. They waved banners at busloads of workers and peasants, and the workers waved back. For their part, the peasants who had come to the city for errands, to visit the hospitals, or to sell their goods at the markets looked terrified. What on earth were the city people up to? Their wide-eyed stares suggested they thought another Cultural Revolution was just around the corner. Seeing their fear, I began to feel afraid too.

By the time we got to the post office, Doug and I were shivering. It was a cold December day, with a biting wind that went straight through our jackets. Riding through the streets on our bikes, I felt the metal frame beneath me like ice. My fingers froze along the handlebars. My nose was running down my lips.

As we lined up at the phone kiosk, suddenly my mind went blank.

"I can't remember my parents' phone number," I gasped.

"What?!" Doug glanced over his shoulder at the crowd of demonstrators chanting on the sidewalk. "Just relax, just calm down, don't worry," he said, nervously licking his lips, his eyes blinking rapidly. "Just don't panic."

"You're making me nervous." I closed my eyes and tried to think. My parents had just moved that fall with my brother to Laramie, Wyoming, but now all I could think of was their old number in South Dakota. I couldn't even think of the Wyoming area code.

"Did you write it down somewhere?" Doug blew on his fingers. He was hopping up and down on his toes, trying to keep warm. I ignored him and tried to concentrate. I let my mind go blank, I didn't think of the demonstrators, the faint but persistent rhythm of their chants, I closed my ears to Doug's entreaties. Numbers swirled through my mind, and then, suddenly, it came to me.

"Got it!" I called out, and I was able to call home.

I woke my parents from a sound sleep in the middle of the night. My father answered the phone. "Whaa—?" he muttered, still half asleep.

"Papa, it's me. I'm still in Nanjing. There are riots here. Demonstrators. You have to call the embassy."

"Jeff?" My father yawned.

"No!" I hissed. "Put Mama on the phone!"

I could hear the sheets rustle as my father turned over in bed. As he handed the phone to my mother, I could hear him say, "Here. It's Jeff. In China." And then he fell back to sleep with a snore.

Fortunately, my mother was wide awake and took the message. She promised me she'd call all the authorities, even my school. She'd make sure something was done about the situation. I was infinitely relieved.

As Doug and I prepared to ride back to the university, he was excited, high from our success. We had braved the streets, waded among the demonstrators, called for help, and survived to tell the tale. But me, I was pissed. "I can't believe my father called me Jeff!" I complained. "I just can't believe it!"

That evening the demonstrations increased in size. Some of the Chinese students in our dorm ventured out and reported that they'd seen people walking ten abreast down the middle of Zhong Shan Boulevard. Buses had been stopped. "This time, they're shouting 'Liberty! Liberty! We want liberty!'" A new group of demonstrators was now taking to the streets. If the first group had been profoundly racist and xenophobic, this group called for an investigation into the so-called 12-24 Riot. They were protesting against official corruption. They too carried banners that said Chinese were second-class citizens in their own country, but they wanted reforms rather than a return to the past. No one was using the word "democracy" yet, but their meaning was clear. They wanted the government to be accountable to its people.

There had been bona fide pro-democracy demonstrations in Nanjing in 1986 and 1987, but the local government had cracked down on them quickly. Student journals and magazines had been shut down. A few students had been expelled. Stiffer sentences were promised in the future. Such actions had stopped the demonstrations for a year, but now, emboldened by the success of the anti-foreigner demonstrators, the pro-reform students were taking to the streets again.

Our Chinese roommates were all very excited by this turn of events. Some of them decided to join the demonstrations, though others felt they should stay and protect us in case things turned around again. The anti-foreigner demonstrators felt outnumbered by the new pro-reform groups and had disappeared from around our dorms sometime around sunset, but there was no telling when they might return.

That evening, the kid from Texas approached me and asked if I would teach his English classes. He was afraid to venture outside anymore after the incident with his camera that afternoon.

"I'll give you my pay," he promised.

"I don't need your money," I said, rather huffily. I was still rather sore about the unequal salaries.

"Look, it's not for me. I need you to help my students." Then he explained that this was the last night of class, and he was supposed to give them oral proficiency exams. If they passed, the school would give them a certificate saying they had taken such-and-such English class and succeeded. The problem was that many of the students were poor workers and had been forced to pay for the class with their own money. They were trying to get extra training to keep their jobs. But if they passed the exam, their work units would pay them back. "They don't have a lot of money," he said. "They need this certificate."

Finally, I agreed to do it. I figured I'd already made it out and back in daylight. Surely, in the dark, everyone would think I was Chinese. There shouldn't be any problems from the demonstrators.

So I found myself bicycling through the cold night air to his school, where indeed his students had been anxiously awaiting his arrival. They were rather surprised to see me instead of their teacher, but the director of the school knew me, and he assured them that I was American and that the school would accept my grades.

The guy from Texas had already told me I should pass everyone, so the exams went fairly smoothly. I discovered that the students were reluctant to leave once they were finished, however. They wanted to talk to me about their lives, their work, their anxieties about the future. "I'm too old to learn new things. But I must. I don't want to lose my job," one man sighed. They all echoed his anxieties. They understood that now that China had opened up to the West, their world was going to change very rapidly. And they were afraid they would be unable to compete.

It was well after eleven when I set off for the dorms. Normally the streets were quiet and mostly deserted by this time, just a few bicyclists darting here and there, people returning from a late shift at work. But this night the streets were thronged with people. The students were out in full force, carrying candles, flashlights, even torches. They held aloft beautiful red banners with gold and black calligraphy. Some of them I could read: Reform! Open to the West! Chinese citizens first! Others fluttered in the breeze and flickered like flames. Some of the students chanted, others sang. I followed one group down a cobblestone alley, behind the Ming Dynasty drum tower at the center of the city. Door to door, they passed out hand-printed pamphlets, detailing the kind of reforms they wanted, startling the residents of the traditional brick houses that still crowded the narrow back streets of Nanjing in those days. I noticed that other people like me were riding behind the demonstrators, wide-eyed and curious, weaving to and fro, trying to see what was going on.

In the distance, just beneath the boisterous singing and the wind whistling through the bare sycamore trees, I could hear a faint rumbling sound. I didn't know what it was, but I noticed that the students picked up their pace and then suddenly disappeared into a courtyard. The other bicyclists suddenly sped up and I realized that I had no idea where I was. I had followed the demonstrators for miles. Before I could be left alone in the dark, narrow alley, I decided to follow a man whizzing past me on a Flying Pigeon, bent low over his handlebars, peddling as though his life depended on it. It was all I could do to keep up with him as he bobbed in and out of puddles of light from distant streetlamps and the faint glow of the neon signs that signaled we had entered a more commercial district. Finally he turned back toward a main street and I began to get my bearings. I was not far from the university. Maybe half a mile or so.

By the time we merged onto Zhong Shan Boulevard, I realized that the rumbling was coming from tanks that were slowly making their way down the far southern end of the boulevard. Soldiers already lined the streets, linking arms, as students demonstrating on the sidewalks tried to break through the human chain. The boulevard had cleared of all vehicles, no cars, buses, or trucks, leaving just me and few dozen other bicyclists who looked as startled and panicked as I felt. Soldiers were shouting into bullhorns, students were chanting.

Then I saw him. A soldier with a rifle slung over his shoulder, standing in the middle of the street. He was waving his arms at some bicyclists, directing traffic, as it were, and then he picked up a bullhorn and began shouting something into the air.

His voice distorted by the wind and the amplification of the bullhorn, he might as well have been speaking in Greek. I had no idea what he was saying. Suddenly he was looking directly at me and shouting.

I didn't know what to do.

I realized I looked completely Chinese in the dark. I was wearing Chinese clothes and riding a Chinese-made bicycle, a little pink Swan brand.

What if he doesn't know I'm a foreigner and thinks I'm deliberately disobeying? What if I make a wrong move? Will he shoot me?

I thought about turning around in the middle of the street and heading back in the opposite direction, but that's where the tanks were coming from. My legs kept pedaling independently of my mind. I thought maybe I would just ride past this man, when suddenly he came running toward me, grabbed my handlebars, and forcibly turned my bike so that I had to ride off into an alley that I hadn't noticed before. And then I realized, that's what he had wanted. He was trying to clear Zhong Shan Boulevard.

Fortunately, I was close enough to the university now to know how to find my way back to the school using back roads. I peddled like crazy until I was home. The gatekeeper recognized me and opened the tall, wooden university gates, then locked them quickly behind me.

Five months later, student demonstrations at Tiananmen Square, in Beijing, would also end when the army was called in, but in violence, whereas in Nanjing not a shot was fired.

I returned to Nanjing that fall, this time on a year-long teaching fellowship, and heard all about what had happened after I'd left. By now, because of the violence at Tiananmen, martial law had been declared, and no one was demonstrating about anything. I heard that one worker was sentenced to ten years in prison for breaking a bowl during a demonstration, but the authorities had been lenient with the students. All my friends agreed that this was a case of "killing the rooster to scare the monkey." It was too bad for the worker, they said, shaking their heads, but it was better than what had happened at Tiananmen.

The African students were back in a new dormitory. Nobody knew if there had been an investigation into the corrupt officials who had taken their money (not to mention organized the riot), but at least this year they were receiving their stipends on time and in full.

Oddly enough, I found that the whole experience helped me to put my years in South Dakota in perspective. In Nanjing, the riot and the subsequent demonstrations had shown me that the same anxieties were being experienced around the world. There were people everywhere who were afraid of interracial dating, people who disliked other races, people who feared change and the uncertain future that such change heralded. The xenophobic demonstrations revealed the deep anxiety some people in China had of falling behind and their desire to return to a familiar past. Even if that past had been filled with poverty and unhappiness, at least these were familiar things. And yet the demonstrations had also given me a lot of reasons to have hope. While thugs had destroyed the Africans' dorms, chased them, lobbed stones at them, other Chinese people had shown remarkable courage. They had tried to shelter the African students that night in their own homes. They brought food to them when they were housed in the railway station. Students had called for an investigation into the corrupt officials. There had been so many people demonstrating in favor of more openness, more contacts with the world, reform. They were not afraid of the future.

And I saw my years in South Dakota as being shaped by these same forces. My neighbors' fear of change, of economic uncertainty, of racial anxiety, of the unknowable future compared to the known past, were the same as China's.

And I realized, finally, that it had not been my fault. The Africans had not deserved to be attacked, just as my family had not deserved to be attacked. We were all unique individuals, yet we had been labeled as some kind of enemy so easily, so quickly, we hadn't seen it coming. Black Devils. Foreign Devils. Japs. Chinks.

Sometimes we are in the wrong place at the wrong time. Sometimes we witness history without understanding the forces of change that are unfolding around us.

25

The End of Staring

Once I had left home at age eighteen, I did not come home for Thanksgiving, although I did return for Christmas, when the dorms closed and all students were forced to leave campus. At home, I worked on the farm again and in my mother's photography studio, but after my freshman year I also made sure that I applied for summer jobs and internships so that I wouldn't have to come home for more than a few weeks. I went on two study-abroad programs and did not return for any holidays while I was out of the country. I lived in France, Hong Kong, China, Taiwan. During the summer, I worked as a copyeditor for a newspaper in Kansas City, Missouri, and as a reporter in Des Moines, Iowa, for the Associated Press, with whom I would eventually become a full-fledged newswoman. I returned to China after the Tiananmen Square massacre, after martial law had been declared across the country, despite my mother's fears.

In the meantime, my family was left to cope with their trials without me.

Since I'd stopped coming home, they had to pare down the farm. They sold the cows, then most of the meat chickens without ordering a new batch, and finally the layers were allowed to grow old. One of my brother's new dogs killed quite a few of them, and my family decided to let the egg business fall by the wayside. They sold the goats that my mother had loved so much. After my senior year in high school, they had given up on pigs entirely.

My brother started college locally, where he was at first mistaken for a Native American student. The head of the local Bureau of Indian Affairs called my brother into his office one afternoon. "So, Jeff," the man smiled pleasantly, "what tribe are you?"

But my brother didn't have a tribe and had to find his own way to fit into the university. There were enormous fights, one involving a fraternity house of drunken pledges, but my brother was able to make new friends, from Iowa and other neighboring states, young men who hadn't been raised to fear people who looked a little different from themselves.

There were still some shootings, although by now most people in town and on the neighboring farms knew my family so well that they didn't feel as threatened as before. My mother's beloved dog, Tiger, was killed in the driveway one June. He had been a Mother's Day gift from my brother. For my part, I had merely sent a card to her from another country, I forget which one, and it had arrived late.

Eventually, however, all the administrators who had despised my father, who had been jealous of him, who had resented him, left the university, and the new administration began to give him credit for the innovations that he had suggested, which were finally being implemented.

When I was a junior, in 1988, my father found a new job as an administrator at the University of Wyoming. My family packed all summer long—I only vaguely remember their letters and postcards. I wasn't there to help, of course. I was in Kansas City for my newspaper internship. Then, by the time they needed to move to Laramie, I had returned to China for my study-abroad program. Because of the tight schedule between the end of my job and my flight out of the country, I hadn't lifted a finger to help them.

I remember the first letter I received from my brother from "our" new home in Wyoming. He wrote to me in Nanjing, a letter that began: "Dear May-lee, You won't believe this!! Nobody stares at us here. Dad and I went all over town, and nobody stared."

At first, my parents were still very worried, because they had still been unable to find a buyer for the South Dakota farm. And then, by a stroke of luck, their carpet cleaner won the Iowa State Lottery and was able to pay cash for the farm, no need for any bank loans. They had to sell it for ten thousand dollars less than they'd paid, despite all the improvements—the barns, the screen porch, the new plumbing, the additional fields they'd purchased and that my mother, brother, and I had personally cleared of the dreaded cocklebur weed. But they accepted the man's offer. He said he'd fallen in love with the place while cleaning the carpets. My father was disappointed that they were losing money. Real estate was supposed to be a sound investment. But my mother told him that they should take the deal. "It's an act of God," she exclaimed. "How many more people are going to win that lottery and want to buy our house?"

My mother's faith had remained unshaken despite the years of turmoil we had experienced.

26

Fear Itself

It seems ridiculous now, the fear Americans in the 1980s and early '90s used to have of the Japanese. I remember Yoshi Hattori, the Japanese high school exchange student who was shot to death in Louisiana when he knocked on the wrong door while looking for a Halloween party. And the best-seller, *Rising Sun.* Japanese businessmen weren't content to wage war economically on America, they wanted our white women, too—for kinky sex and murder. Then there was poor Vincent Chin, the Chinese American engineer who was mistaken for a Japanese and beaten to death by an unemployed auto worker and his friend in Detroit in 1982. "It's because of you motherfuckers we're out of work!" one of the men shouted, according to witnesses. In return for pleading guilty and no contest, respectively, to beating Vincent Chin to death, Ronald Ebens and Michael Nitz received three years' probation and were fined $3,780.[10]

When I was going to college in Iowa, the *Des Moines Register* op-ed page led the charge against the supposed Japanese invasion of America. As one letter writer put it, "Wake up, America. Japan is taking over the country more every day."[11] A regular columnist was con-

[10]Helen Zia, *Asian American Dreams: The Emergence of an American People* (New York: Farrar, Straus and Giroux, 2000), 60.

[11]Letter to the editor, "Sold to Japanese," *Des Moines Register,* June 26, 1989, 9A.

vinced that a war was already under way. In a column entitled "The Latest War with Japan," Donald Kaul wrote, "Japan has achieved its economic victories at the expense of its citizens, who work hard and live poor so that their corporations can be rich. They take it as their patriotic duty. Just as though they were at war."[12] In another column, he warned against a U.S.-Japanese joint venture to design a new fighter plane, concluding grimly, "We've forgotten Pearl Harbor."[13]

It all seems so sadly absurd at the beginning of the twenty-first century.

Sometimes I wonder if the people who warned us that the Japanese were going to wage war on us, take over our country, and destroy our economy feel guilty today. Perhaps they have forgotten the hysteria of the '80s and moved on with their lives, like the Symbionese Liberation Army activist who became a housewife and cookbook author in Minnesota. They have drifted off into suburban comfort. They have found other ways to occupy their time. Or perhaps they are too busy warning us about a "clash of civilization" with Muslims. There are always opportunities for fearmongers. There are papers to sell, ratings to think about. A trade war with China? North Korean nukes? Mexicans crossing the Sonora Desert? In a few more decades, will we be told it's the Vietnamese who are out to get us all over again?

I used to wonder if all the anti-Japanese fearmongering in the media was in part responsible for the hostility we faced in the '80s. When a man yelled "Jap" out the window of his pickup at me, was he really afraid that I represented some kind of Asian takeover of his town? Or was his fear so visceral he couldn't analyze where it had come from?

I'm a grown woman now, in my thirties, but it still hurts to think about those years I spent growing up in South Dakota. At the same time, distance has made those events, the exaggerated fears that

[12] Donald Kaul, "Over the Coffee: The Latest War with Japan," *Des Moines Register,* April 21, 1989, 15A.

[13] Donald Kaul, "Over the Coffee: The Things We Are Forgetting," *Des Moines Register,* March 22, 1989.

people could have about the likes of me and my family, seem surreal, almost comical.

Recently I've been reading articles about people undergoing genetic tests to trace their ancestry, Y-chromosomes and mitochondrial DNA, and the shock they express when the results come back more mixed than they had imagined. One writer who had always assumed he was African American discovered that he was 57 percent Indo-European, 39 percent Native American, and 4 percent East Asian. "I was floored," the man told *Newsweek.*[14] The *New York Times* reported that a hundred students in an ethnic studies class at Penn State took genetic tests to determine their heritage. One student with two black parents discovered he was 48 percent European. Many students who thought they were white discovered they were not exactly European Americans but that they too were "mixed." "Shocked" was how some students expressed their reaction to the findings.

Shocked and awed. And, for some, even excited.[15]

[14]Claudia Kalb, "In Our Blood," *Newsweek*, February 6, 2006, 55.

[15]Emma Daly, "DNA Tells Students They Aren't Who They Thought," *New York Times*, April 13, 2005.

27

The Family Trees

As I began writing our story, I found myself unexpectedly living at midlife with my father, and in Wyoming. I had left my snug apartment in San Francisco (right on the 1-California line, exactly halfway between the two Chinatowns, twenty minutes in four directions to twenty-two movie screens, a ten-minute walk to two Thai restaurants and one Korean barbecue joint). But my father—a widower now—had injured himself, and so I dropped everything to take care of him while he underwent physical therapy.

It was because of my mother's trees that he was now in this predicament. Russian olives, to be exact. My mother had planted them a dozen years earlier, but then the previous May a late spring storm blew in from Cody and dumped some eight inches of heavy wet snow on the town of Laramie. It had been an unusually warm spring and the trees were already in full bloom, adorned not with tight buds or blossoms but with dense canopies of leaves. The boughs began to bend under the snow, then to creak, then, as the wind picked up, to break. My father heard the first snap in his study, where he was trying to grade the last of his students' exams. He hurried from his desk to the window, parting the curtains to peer into the swirling snowflakes. It took a minute for his eyes to adjust to the intense white light. And then he saw very clearly: the injured tree, its limb dragging against the earth like a broken wing. It seemed to shiver in the cold, all its frosted leaves trembling unhappily.

A strange creaking noise filled the air, just audible beneath the howling of the wind. It was an old, arthritic sound. If his knees could talk, my father said, this was exactly what they'd sound like.

He realized the trees were going to die. The snow would break their heavy boughs, and they'd never recover. The climate in Laramie is arid, as the city rests on a plateau between two mountain ranges, 7,200 feet above sea level. There is little precipitation, the wind is fierce, the winters long, the sunlight harsh. The trees grew slowly. When my parents first moved to this town, my mother was shocked by the austerity of the lawn and went out to buy saplings—a grove of aspens, seven evergreens, and two Russian olives—to protect the house from the strong, cold winds. It had taken the trees twelve and a half years to grow to a respectable height. Now they were in imminent danger, and soon there might be nothing left but my father's memories of them.

He grabbed his coat and the broom from the kitchen and rushed out into the storm. I could picture him, teeth gritted, beating the snow from the trees' branches, brushing the wet slush from the lower boughs, then reaching higher, swinging the broom back and forth against the leafy upper branches, knocking the snow to the ground in mini-avalanches. Snow fell against his glasses, he said, down the back of his neck. He felt itchy all over as the snow burned against his skin, but he wasn't going to give up. He would save my mother's trees, all right. He wasn't going to let a little spring snow destroy thirteen years of growth.

He was swinging away, his heart racing, the blood rushing through his veins, when suddenly he heard a little pop! in his back. At first it felt like a tiny balloon in his spine had been pricked with a pin. And then the real pain hit.

Oh, god, oh, god, oh, god! What a fool I've been! he thought. And all for what? For trees? For lousy, scrawny, good-for-nothing trees!

He put his left hand to the small of his back. He planted the broom against the ground and held tight with his right hand. He took a step. Pain shot through his left leg, circled through the ankle joint, and coursed back up his thigh. He wanted to cry.

The worst part was how stupid he felt.

Through sheer power of will he trudged through the snow and made it back inside the house. He was drenched in sweat, could barely see straight, was conscious only of the blood exploding in his head, pounding in his temples in rhythm with the pain radiating up and down his left leg and throbbing in his back. For a moment he thought he was having a heart attack, but he couldn't even make it to the phone. He stumbled into the warmth of the kitchen, his glasses fogging up immediately, dropped the broom, stumbled toward the dining room, tripped over the broom, and tumbled to the floor. He landed on his knees, which sent another electric pulse of pain so great through his entire body that he would have welcomed death. Instead, he stretched out onto the floor, lay flat on his back, and dared not move until the pain in his back and leg and knee and hip subsided.

At that moment, my father realized he had become an old man. He was so startled by this revelation that for a full minute he felt no pain, only astonishment.

After he called the doctor, he called me. And of course I came, because I did not want to lose another parent, not so soon after my mother's death from cancer. No matter how many years have passed since her death, it still feels as though she has only just recently passed away. I have to catch myself when I talk to people who don't know my family—I find myself still referring to my "parents" plural, and sometimes I still speak of my mother in present tense. My friends are used to these quirks, but I've found it can be confusing to strangers.

Now my father was undergoing physical therapy for a herniated disk and I found myself in my parents' house, the one I hadn't grown up in, the one where I'd never even had a bed, the one they'd moved to while I was living in China and determined never to return home.

My father's neighbors, strangers to me, flocked to wish him well. They cooed over him in the grocery store parking lot, in the check-out lanes at the Super Wal-Mart and Big K. And to each he told the story of his desire to become a tree.

"I'm too old," he'd say, milking their sympathy shamelessly. "I don't have any regrets. I've led an exciting life. But for my next life, I want to be a tree." (He'd decided recently, he told me, to return to his Buddhist roots. Apparently quite literally.)

"What kind of tree?" I demanded. "Deciduous? Spruce? Pine? *Russian olive?*" I said the last bit with deliberate irony, but my father pretended not to understand.

"Yup," he told his wide-eyed neighbors—they were not used to this kind of talk in Laramie, Wyoming. He nodded with satisfaction. "It's going to be a tree for me from now on."

When we were alone, however, my father assured me that he had not forgotten his promise to my mother.

"What promise?" I asked.

"I told her I would find her. No matter where in the universe her soul went, I would find her again. And she said, 'I know you will.' She believed me." He nodded proudly.

I couldn't respond then. I had no words to express what I felt, the jagged edges of glass that had shattered in my heart.

I knew that if I was to keep my sanity and not collapse from grief and too many memories, I had to keep busy. But it was the middle of a Laramie winter. The harsh, insistent winds kept me indoors. Just walking around the block left my cheeks so frozen that I could not feel them for half an hour after I came back inside. So I decided that I would clean the house. My father had not touched my mother's closet, although she had died five years earlier. Or her dresser. A single white knit glove lay at an angle on the polished wooden top, just as she must have left it. Her art room was filled with paintings and photographs in jumbled piles. Her books still had markers in them. Her reading glasses, coated with dust, lay unfolded before her computer, which was shrouded beneath a green embroidered tablecloth.

Everywhere I looked, there were reminders of my mother. Even the blue address book remained organized as she would have preferred, friends and relatives recorded under their first names or nicknames, rather than alphabetized by surname.

"How can you live like this?" I asked my father once in exasperation.

"Like what?" he answered.

And I knew then that it was up to me to change things. My mother, I knew, would not have approved of this type of enshrinement of her discarded relics.

At first the sheer monumental scope of the task gave me the energy to bag clothes for the Goodwill, to dust and vacuum, organize and stack, to go through file after file from her business before throwing them away, just to make sure I wasn't discarding something we might still need. Like the picture of our family I found tucked among old bills. Or the ad clipped from the newspaper that showed our old farm in South Dakota, the farm that had been her dream house and the source of so many nightmares for me.

But then, slowly, over the weeks and months, I began to dream of my mother. I hadn't dreamed of her for years, not since the year she died, when I dreamed about her almost nightly: she was always in pain then, calling out to me, but when I rushed to her bedside, she merely rocked back and forth, mutely, and I was unable to offer any form of solace. Now my dreams were different. My mother was not the cancer patient I had nursed for two years, but rather the vibrant, healthy, smiling woman I had grown up with. In these new dreams she was always talking, waving her long-fingered hands in the air, sunlight streaming into her blonde hair so that it shone. She was happy, she was driving her Jeep, a camera at her side, and we were going on some new adventure. Sometimes I was a child again, and sometimes I was myself, a grown woman, only a few years younger than my mother. But when I woke each morning the real nightmare began, because as I lay in bed between dreams and consciousness, I would have to remember, day after day, dawn after dawn, that my mother was dead, and that my dream was only that.

Each morning as I woke, I cried. Then I washed my face and pretended I was fine, as my father hobbled about the house, one hand on his sore back, and I set about cleaning with even more fury than before.

It was many bags of trash, endless rolls of paper towels, and several cans of Pledge later that I finally discovered my mother's secret files, the ones that contained her writing. That is where I found the synopsis for the novel she was planning to write. She had enrolled in some kind of mail-order writing course, with a "real published author" as mentor. In her prospectus she described the novel she wanted to write. Her book was to be about a mixed-race family that moves from the New York metropolitan area to rural South Dakota and is attacked savagely by local bigots. In the novel, the family overcomes all difficulties and the story ends well, triumphantly even, with the family moving on with their life, succeeding in all manner of businesses and endeavors.

What surprised me was the phrase "the children faced real, physical danger on a daily basis," because until this moment, five years after my mother's death, I had never really been certain what my mother knew about my brother's and my experiences in South Dakota. She had never mentioned them. Nor had my father. In fact, we used to argue, he and I, vehemently, about our life in South Dakota, my father insisting that it was all our fault if we had troubles in school and in town and wherever we went in between.

"There's no such thing as racism against Chinese!" he'd declare. "You just don't know how to get along with people!"

And I remembered immediately the feeling I got, deep in my gut, everything there tightening, as though preparing my body for another blow. Even after we stopped arguing, stopped shouting at the dinner table, stopped talking entirely, I still felt that clenched, expectant tightening in my whole body.

For all their many wonderful qualities, my parents were never able to discuss race with my brother and me. They were not able to talk to us about why people stared at us in town. Why they stared at my parents, a Chinese man with a blonde woman. Even after the shootings began, after our pets were killed and left for us to find in the driveway, my parents could find no words to explain what was happening, and in some way I think my brother and I learned to blame ourselves. In fact, I know this to be true. I just never wanted to admit it.

But now, upon finding my mother's two-page outline for a novel (one she never actually finished), I knew that she knew. And suddenly I felt such relief, a feeling of warmth rushing through my entire body, as though I had plunged into a warm pool of water. I didn't even realize I was crying until my father found me sitting on the floor of my mother's art room, surrounded by empty Pledge cans and paper towels and Hefty bags.

"What's the matter?" he asked, genuinely alarmed, his eyes growing wide behind his glasses.

"Nothing," I said, startled. "Why?"

Then he shuffled down the hall, his slippers flapping one way and the other, and he returned with a box of Kleenex, and that's when I realized that my face was wet, my glasses fogged, snot pooling around my upper lip.

And so I began to write about things I thought I would never tell another soul as long as I lived, because I realized that my mother would have wanted me to do so. I would not be embarrassing my family, as I had felt for so many years. I would, at last, be telling the story of how our mixed-race family moved from the New York metropolitan area to a rural community fearful of change, were attacked savagely, yet found a way to survive.

Acknowledgments

I have changed the names of all my junior high and high school classmates. My mother's dear friend, Mary Imelda Lynch, is named in full, as I believe this is what they both would have wanted. Public figures' real names are used throughout.

In writing this book, I found a number of works useful in helping me to understand the context surrounding our experiences in South Dakota. First and foremost is Peter Matthiessen's account of the Leonard Peltier trial and violence on the Pine Ridge Reservation in the 1970s, *In the Spirit of Crazy Horse* (New York: Penguin Books, 1992). An op-ed piece of interest was "Janklow: Fall of a South Dakota Hero" by Josh Garrett-Davis (*Denver Post,* October 20, 2003, 7B). Also useful was "DLN Issues: Jancita Eagle Deer, Disbarment Opinion," found on the website of the Dakota-Lakota-Nakota Human Rights Advocacy Coalition, http://www.dlncoalition.org/dln_issues/janklowdisbarment opinion.htm. Other useful sources on politics, public perception, the media, and racial violence include Helen Zia's *Asian American Dreams: The Emergence of an American People* (New York: Farrar, Straus and Giroux, 2000); Donald Kaul's series of anti-Japanese columns in the *Des Moines Register* ("Over the Coffee") during the spring of 1989; *Asian Americans and Politics,* edited by Gordon H. Chang (Stanford: Stanford University Press, 2001); *Re/Collecting Early Asian America: Essays in Cultural History,* edited by Josephine Lee, Imogene L. Lim, and Yuko Matsukawa (Philadelphia: Temple University Press, 2002) (especially Yuko Matsukawa's essay "Representing the Oriental in Nineteenth-Century Trade Cards"); Najia Aarim-Heriot's *Chinese Immigrants, African Americans, and Racial Anxiety in the United States, 1848–82* (Urbana: University of Illinois Press, 2003); and Mary Ting Yi Lui's *The Chinatown Trunk Mystery: Murder, Miscegenation, and Other Dangerous Encounters in Turn-of-the Century New York City* (Princeton: Princeton University Press, 2005).

Finally, in addition to my father's own memories, documents, papers, and student publications and his colleagues' notes from City College of New York, which I discovered stored in boxes in his basement, I found through interlibrary loan two books that were useful in providing context about City College, although they are not always in keeping with my father's views and impressions of that institution. They are *Academic Turmoil: The Reality and Promise of Open Education,* by Theodore L. Gross (Garden City, N.Y.: Anchor Press/Doubleday, 1980), and *City on a Hill: Testing the American Dream at City College,* by James Traub (New York: Addison-Wesley, 1995).

For the definition of *hapa* on the dedication page, I used the *Asian American Journalists Association Handbook,* which can be downloaded from their website, http://www.aaja.org/resources/apa_handbook.

I would like to thank my former students (all excellent writers and brilliant to boot): Tiffany Chiang, Alex Clark, Penelope Dane, Fadia Hasan (and "Che"), Amy Lehrmitt, George Lew, Jeff Skiles, and Jia-Jia Zhu, for participating in an early reading from this manuscript on the campus of the University of Massachusetts, Amherst, in the spring of 2005 while I was the Visiting Writer at Amherst College. Their enthusiastic input was more useful than they probably realize. Special thanks to writers Sabina Murray and Marilyn Krysl for their insightful comments on early drafts of the manuscript and for their encouragement, as well as Dr. Phylis Lan Lin, executive director of the University of Indianapolis Press, who first published an essay I wrote about my South Dakota experiences, portions of which appear in *Hapa Girl* in somewhat different form. The essay, "Yellow Peril," appeared in my book *Glamorous Asians: Short Stories and Essays* (Indianapolis: University of Indianapolis Press, 2004).

With deepest gratitude I thank my family for putting up with my questions, my endless drafts, and my dogged determination to probe their memories no matter how unhappy this may sometimes have made them. I could not have written this book without the assistance of Jeff Chai and Winberg Chai.

Finally, I would like to thank Janet M. Francendese at Temple University Press and the two anonymous reviewers, who made excellent suggestions for improving the book.

May-lee Chai is the author of three books, *My Lucky Face, The Girl from Purple Mountain* (co-authored with Winberg Chai), and *Glamorous Asians: Short Stories & Essays,* and recipient of an NEA Grant in Literature.